SEXIST RELIGION AND WOMEN IN THE CHURCH

Contributors to This Book

Nelle Morton

Letty M. Russell

Theressa Hoover

Gwen Kennedy Neville

Dorothy D. Burlage

Krister Stendahl

Mary Daly

Gail B. Shulman

Alice L. Hageman

Beverly Wildung Harrison

SEXIST RELIGION AND WOMEN IN THE CHURCH

No More Silence!

Edited by

ALICE L. HAGEMAN

in collaboration with

THE WOMEN'S CAUCUS OF HARVARD DIVINITY SCHOOL

ASSOCIATION PRESS / NEW YORK

SEXIST RELIGION AND WOMEN IN THE CHURCH

Association Press, 291 Broadway, New York, N.Y. 10007

International Standard Book Number:
0-8096-1840-0 (hardbound)
0-8096-1882-6 (paperback)
Library of Congress Catalog Card Number: 73-21672

Library of Congress Cataloging in Publication Data

Hageman, Alice L comp.
Sexist religion and women in the church, no more silence!

Includes bibliographical references.
CONTENTS: Hageman, A. L. Introduction: no more silence!—Morton, N. Preaching the word.—Russell, L. M. Women and ministry. [etc.]
1. Women and religion. I. Title.
BL458.H33 291.1'7834'12 73-21672
ISBN 0-8096-1840-0
ISBN 0-8096-1882-6 (pbk.)

PRINTED IN THE UNITED STATES OF AMERICA

to our foremothers

CONTENTS

FOREWORD/FORWARD!

Theological education has remained an exclusively male domain throughout the many centuries since Mary, Martha's sister, was criticized for listening to Jesus' teaching instead of helping with the refreshments. Although, during the suffrage struggle, some American women found ways to educate themselves and to form their own judgments of religious attitudes toward women, schools that prepare people for professions related to religion have only gradually begun seriously to include women. Late among these, Harvard Divinity School finally opened its doors to non-male students in 1955. As of June, 1973, a meager total of seventy-nine women had received degrees. Until the fall of 1972, representation of women on the faculty of Harvard Divinity School could scarcely be described even as token.

In 1970, the year the Women's Institute of the Boston Theological Institute was created to bring a radical feminist perspective to the study of religion, women studying at Harvard Divinity School gathered for mutual support and to consider women's unequal participation in the school. As the enrollment of women increased during the ensuing years, this informal group developed into a Women's Caucus, meeting weekly to plan political and educational strategy. With a membership of candidates in various degree programs, the Caucus spans perspectives ranging from "soft feminist" to "religious anarchist." Uniting the disparate members is a commitment to challenge patriarchal dominance—political, spiritual, and intellectual. Believing that *de facto* sexism occurring within and structured into religious institutions is heresy, we hope to expose, challenge, and overcome such personal and institutional injustice as we seek to open new possibilities for women and for theology in and out of the churches.

Working out this commitment, we found weekly meetings with the Dean effective in keeping our interests in the forefront of the school's concerns. Other tactics included taking over classes, organizing independent colloquia and fieldwork projects specifically related to women, and founding WITCH, the Women's Inspirational Theological Coalition from Harvard.

Neglect of perspectives and concerns arising from the female half of humanity in the established curriculum left us the task of financing and developing educational opportunities which the school did not offer. Volunteering their time and effort while continuing their own studies, women secured from the Lentz Lecture Fund the means for a lecture series on Women and Religion in 1972–73. Five women and a faculty member conducted a search for someone who would coordinate the series, strategize for the future of Women's Studies at Harvard Divinity School, and teach two courses. The women's work still not done, Caucus members cooperated in the time-consuming and difficult tasks of planning the series, preparing for the unprecedented seminars "Women and Religion in Sexist Society" and "Women and Ministry," and developing a comprehensive proposal for the future of Women's Studies.

Lecturers were chosen to provide the school with the rare opportunity of listening to a number of women scholars. The series reflected a rich variety of perceptions, and a further range of issues, including Gay Liberation, developed in the accompanying seminars. Although we planned and publicized the program as education for the whole community, only a handful of the many male students and faculty attended any of the lectures, except for the one given by a man.

Regardless of male indifference and backlash, the whole process has meant much more to us than we can re-create here. New ways of working together, of understanding ourselves as women, and of relating to each other as sisters were evoked; and out of the intensive intellectual vigor of the seminars and their challenging confrontation with the realities of the church, synagogue, and society developed many exciting papers and continuing projects.

This volume contains the lectures and one of the significant and provocative papers written for the seminar on "Women and Religion in Sexist Society." We are convinced that women can no longer remain silent, each one bearing in isolation the heartrending discouragement of exclusion, suppression, and relegation to woman's traditional place. Our very language has changed as we have confronted sexist conventions. Groping for words to express experienced realities which men in power are too often glad to deny, we have learned to speak words that can call sisterhood into being.

The Lentz Lectures and related seminars, along with the teaching of Dr. Rosemary Ruether—a member of the Harvard Divinity

School faculty in 1972–73—stimulated interest, thinking, and action regarding women's oppression. The Women's Caucus was able to plan for the future despite the current economic stringencies of educational institutions. In 1973–74, five women, employed as Associates in Research, will explore feminist issues and develop forgotten areas in various theological disciplines. Two women will join the teaching faculty; one will come as a Visiting Professor, and two more will work as Director of Ministerial Studies and Coordinator of Women's Programs. We don't propose our adventur. in communal planning as a model for imitation; but, rather, we hope that it will be, in the words of Mary Daly, an instance of "contagious freedom."

The silence has been broken. We offer these words toward the creation of new life in sisterhood.

THE WOMEN'S CAUCUS

Harvard Divinity School
July 1973

IN APPRECIATION

Thanks to those women at Harvard Divinity School and Boston Theological Institute-related schools who worked to secure the Lentz monies, to prepare the lecture series, and to participate in the seminars—for their interest, enthusiasm, criticism, and support: Susan Andrews, Linda Barufaldi, Christina Bowman, Virginia Buckley, Cynthia Campbell, Emily Culpepper, Elizabeth Hanes-Main, Mary Beth James, Lydia Johnson, Georgianna Landrigan, Brinton Lykes, Jean MacRae, Bonlyn McBride, Hazel Meyners, Diane Miller, Ruth Purtillo, Elizabeth Rice, Yvonne Schaudt, Gail Shulman, Denise Tracy, Elsa Wahlberg, and Margaret Wright.

Thanks also to those Lentz Lecturers who have contributed essays to this book. Unfortunately, three other significant contributions to the series were not available for publication at this time: "Ministry and Liberation: Do Women Have a Future in the Church?" by Brigalia Bam, "Women in Their Menial Roles in the Church," by Saundra Graham, and "The Source of Women's Oppression," by Roberta Salper.

Those women who came to the seminars as resource persons should also be acknowledged: Dorothy Austin, Dorothy Bass, Sr. Mary Christine, Lurline Fowler, Susan Halligan, Polly Laughland, Lee Lindman, Lorraine Potter, Emily Preston, Lynn Rhodes, Molly Shera, Nan Stone, and Anne Walsh. From their work as parish ministers, church educators, campus ministers, hospital and prison chaplains, community organizers, church historians, and psychologists, and from their experiences as women in ministry, they contributed greatly to shaping our understanding of both the institutional and personal dimensions of the issues of Women and Ministry!

Special appreciation goes to those women who have helped with the often tedious tasks of preparing this manuscript for publication: Christina Bowman for her work in copy editing; Jean MacRae, Elizabeth Rice, and Gail Shulman, for their work in editorial revision.

Finally, I wish to acknowledge Polly Allen-Robinson's contribution to this book as constant friend, critic, counselor, and sister student of the whys and maybes of our lives as Christian women.

A. L. H.

INTRODUCTION:
No More Silence!

Alice L. Hageman

> Let a woman learn in silence, with all submissiveness. I permit no woman to teach or to have authority over men; she is to keep silent. (I TIMOTHY 2:11–12)

In 1963, Horace DeY. Lentz left to his alma mater, Harvard University, a bequest whose income was to be used "for the giving of one or more lectures every third year by some outstanding Christian priest, minister or layman upon the inspiring things he may discern in the words: *'Cristo et Ecclesiae'* which appear upon the Harvard Seal." As explained in the Foreword to this book, the women of Harvard Divinity School succeeded in having these funds allocated during the 1972-73 academic year for exploration of the issues of Women and Ministry through a public lecture series and two academic seminars. This present book comes out of that experience and contains the "inspiring [and frequently critical] things" discerned by several women and one man about Christ and the Church past, present, and future, especially affecting the lives of women.

As Lentz Lecturer on Women and Ministry at Harvard during 1972–73, I had responsibility for coordinating the lecture series and teaching the seminars. I also worked with The Women's Caucus of the Harvard Divinity School to formulate proposals for the future of Women's Studies there. Early in our proposal-making I was invited to present to an informal luncheon meeting of the Harvard Divinity School faculty my thoughts about the future of women and Women's Studies at that institution. My experience on that occasion provides one glimpse into why the assertion of *No more silence!* holds such an imperative for women today.

In 1972 women (two) were appointed as members of the teaching faculty of Harvard Divinity School for the first time. In that same year, seventeen years after women had been first admitted to the Divinity School as degree candidates, the proportion of women to men in the student body was still less than one to three. Nevertheless, in view of the recent accession of women to the faculty and the growing number of women students, and certainly in view of the presence and work of thousands and millions of women in the church throughout the past 2,000 years, the proposals did not seem unduly revolutionary: *a*) inclusion of women's concerns in the curriculum, *b*) establishment of a Chair in Women's Studies, and *c*) ultimate parity of women with men among faculty and students. Although I anticipated some resistance to these ideas, I was quite unprepared for the explosion which followed my presentation.

For a long . . . long minute there was dead silence. Then a flood of probing, defensive, hostile questions poured out, focusing particularly on the issues of a possible Chair in Women's Studies and parity of women on the faculty. "We're here to train men for the Christian ministry. What does this proposal have to do with preaching the Gospel and bringing in the Kingdom?" asked one distinguished senior professor, plunging in with apparently unconscious irony. "But if we take seriously your proposals, all of our role definitions will have to change. You know that the church is dependent on volunteers for its survival, and as women go to work that source is drying up," observed another faculty member, revealing (perhaps more clearly than he had intended) the personal and institutional anxieties my presentation had stirred up. "How do we know Women's Studies is a serious discipline? What will be its status in fifty or one hundred years?" asked a third scholar. When I replied that the study of church history along *national* lines might well be a questionable "discipline" also, they responded that I was lucky none of the American church history faculty was there to hear me!

Finally, in an effort to express his sympathy for the issue—and for me, the only woman in this roomful of Harvard academics—a theologian created for us the image of the search for evidence of life in outer space as analogous to the search for information about the experience of women in the churches. "In principle," he said, "anyone in the field of astronomy should be alert to evidence of life in outer space. However, usually each one has a particular project for which he is amassing evidence, and so he might well overlook such indications even were he to find them. Besides, the astronomer, with his present training, probably doesn't even know what to look for! Therefore it is important that someone take on that particular task, that a Chair in the important-but-thus-far-neglected area of the Study of Life in Outer Space be established." He concluded that, for similar reasons, "it probably would be a good thing for us to establish a Chair in Women's Studies here at the Divinity School."

My confreres dissolved with laughter at the analogy, and our gathering quickly ended . . . inconclusively. As someone who was feeling very much as though she had just arrived from some faraway planet, I found the theologian's image apt.

Perhaps the most significant thing about the experience described above is that it is not unique. This story of my lunch with the faculty of Harvard Divinity School in late 1972 can be matched by Christian women around the country, perhaps around the world. The settings vary, from theological seminary to state and national denominational office or assembly to local parish, but the basic message is the same: The experience of women within the churches can be compared to that of creatures from outer space—unknown, unnoticed, possibly irrelevant.

No More Silence!

This exclusion from leadership or even visibility imposed on women in the Judaeo-Christian tradition has lasted for several millennia. But now that silence is being broken, that exclusion challenged. *No more silence!* say the women who have quietly organized the bake sales and bazaars and church dinners while men counted the money and planned programs. *No more silence!* say the women whose intelligence and energies have gone into teaching in Sunday schools while men taught in colleges and seminaries. *No more silence!* say women who seek ordination and full recognition of their capabilities as ministers and priests. *No more silence!* say women who celebrate the ordinary and special events in their lives, but refuse to sing about the "Faith of Our Fathers" or to respond to calls of "Rise Up, O Men of God." *No more silence!* say women who have denied themselves the sensual pleasures of their bodies, fearful of being called "Temptress" or "Daughter of Eve."

No more silence! The silence is being broken by theologians and historians, by ethicists and Biblical scholars, by church executives and lay women, by Protestants and Catholics and Jews. It is being broken in love of the faith—and with the force of centuries of accumulated anger and oppression. It is being broken so that women may discover whether they can in fact express their full humanity within the context of the Christian faith.

Although the determination to say *No more silence!* is now strong and firm and growing, the effort to assess the experience of growing up female and Christian—of hearing and believing the Gospel as women—is still a relatively new venture. Prior to 1967, there was only a handful of such works, written mostly by Europeans related to the World Council of Churches and focused primarily on the question of the ordination of women.[1*] Although there is now a veritable deluge of articles along with an increasing number of books on women in the churches, the first major contributions originating in the United States did not appear until the late 1960's.[2]

In addition to publications, women's centers are springing up around the country. They now include the Women's Theological Coalition of the Boston Theological Institute; the women's center of the Graduate Theological Union in Berkeley, California; the library of Temple University in Philadelphia, with a special collection on women and religion, and the offices of Church Women United in New York City.

Institutions are changing as well. Women's caucuses are developing in various denominations. The General Assembly of the United Presbyterian Church has established a permanent Council on Women and the Church. The Women's Caucus–

* Superior figures refer to section of numbered Notes at end of each article.

Religious Studies, organized by women associated with the American Academy of Religion and the Society for Biblical Literature, publishes a Newsletter with information for women interested in the field of religion. Thus far, however, Union Theological Seminary in New York City is the only seminary in the United States officially to commit itself to parity of women in student body and faculty.

New Developments in the Struggle

The Lentz Lecture Series at Harvard Divinity School in 1972–73 and this book represent one more contribution to the work of breaking the long, long silence of women in Western Christendom. Several of the contributors to this volume can be considered authentic pioneers in both faith and practice. Nelle Morton, for example, has been working steadily for several decades on behalf of women in the churches, and oppressed minorities in church and society. Since 1948 Theressa Hoover has held significant positions within church structures, nationally and internationally. Letty Russell was one of the first three women to be graduated *(cum laude)* from Harvard Divinity School in 1958, and was among the first to break the barrier and be ordained by the United Presbyterian Church. In *The Church and the Second Sex,* published in 1968, Mary Daly provided a critical analysis of the situation of women in the church; in her most recent book *Beyond God the Father: Toward a Philosophy of Women's Liberation* she has moved beyond a focus on the church to a consideration of how the women's movement itself represents a spiritual revolution within our total culture.

Although all but one of the contributors is presently an academic, they have had a variety of other experiences—parish minister, campus minister, church executive, civil rights organizer, international representative, wife and mother, husband and father. Despite the academic halls (a theological seminary) in which these lectures were originally heard, we are hopeful that they will prove to be of utility to people who live their lives in other places and in other contexts.

The offerings of reflection and analysis in the following pages attempt to advance us a few steps in our effort to understand where we come from as women who are related to the Judaeo-Christian tradition, and why we presently are as we are. A closer look at our history, the exposure to the experience of our fore-mothers, helps lay bare our roots. Gail Shulman's treatment of women in the Jewish tradition, Beverly Harrison's consideration of our immediate predecessors in U.S. Protestantism, Theressa Hoover's description of life for black church women in white society, my own probe of the mixed results of women's missionary ventures into foreign lands—all seek to broaden our perception of where we are coming from . . . and of those struggles, successes, and setbacks of our foremothers which have helped shape our options. Krister Stendahl points out the difficulties of joining theory and practice—of translating the rhetoric of equality into implementation of the self-evident justice in the demands which women are making on the churches. Nelle Morton, Dorothy Bur-lage, and Gwen Neville remind us of the ways in which Christian ideology—as operative in our patriarchal culture—conditions our heads, shapes our experience, limits our wanderings, whether con-cerning the exercise of our intellects, delight in our bodies, options for our work, or roles within our families.

Mary Daly and Letty Russell embark on the very difficult, uncharted path of turning our sights to the future—in or out of the churches. Each helps us to assess where we will go next, what we are willing to endure, and what we are willing to give up; they also push us to set goals and to begin to formulate strategies. Must we leave behind the known patterns of an irredeemable institution while still affirming our future life in the Spirit? Can the new wine we drink be poured out of patched and reshaped wineskins, or must the containers be fashioned wholly new? Can or should we transform a dying religion, its institutions and ideologies, into that beloved vision offered in Galatians 3:26–28:

> For in Christ Jesus you are all [children] of God, through faith. For as many of you as were baptized into Christ have put on Christ. There is neither Jew nor Greek, there is neither slave nor free, there is nei-ther male nor female; for you are all one in Christ Jesus.

Issues for the Future

Several issues central to a consideration of women in the

churches and in the society are touched upon but left unresolved in this book. These indicate the scope of the agenda which awaits our further thought and action.

Many crucial questions are raised, especially in the Daly and Hageman essays: Are women a *caste* or a *class?* Is women's oppression the paradigm of all oppression? Are *all* women more oppressed than *all* men? What are the *sources* of women's oppression and the strategies most effective in overcoming it? These are topics which engage the attention of feminists, Marxists, humanists, and philosophers today; these should also be issues of concern to the churches which in principle bring Good News to both women and men, poor and rich, powerless and powerful.

Since very early in the Christian era, the churches have clearly been among the most powerful of the societal forces for subduing women and keeping them in their place. As Burlage points out, the churches have helped to assure legitimacy within patriarchal families and to maintain public standards of morality. In addition, within the churches, as within other heterosexual groupings in this country, women are assigned a role with status inferior to that of men.

Nevertheless, within our male-female caste system, as is indicated perhaps most poignantly in Hoover's essay, there are clear differences of class among women. There are also differences of class between some women (especially upper- and middle-class white women) and some men (lower-class and/or poorly educated minority [especially black] men). A black minister's wife who crosses town to work as a domestic in a white woman's household does share a common oppression with her employer—that of being a woman. Indeed, they may even share a common commitment to the Christian faith. Nevertheless, the other conditions of their lives, their racial and economic and social differences, create a nearly unbridgeable gulf between them. This gulf is marked by greater social, emotional, and economic affinity between the black woman and the black man than between the black woman and the white woman; it possibly even implies advantages for the white woman over the black man.

All women suffer psychic oppression because their sex limits their options in a patriarchal society. Many women *and* many men (some more than others) also experience constant economic, social, and psychic deprivation in their struggle to survive in a hierarchical competitive capitalist society. A few women do "make it," joining men in roles of adjunct oppressors to keep the system going. Unraveling these dynamics of caste and class, of psychic and economic oppression, of sex and race and nation —and showing how they operate—is a monumental intellectual task. Resolving the issue, so that no one is kept in an inferior place because of class or sex, or race, will demand concerted political action.

Another set of issues concerns the relationship between women and ministry. First, can we develop the new forms of ministry (ministry of the *whole* people of God and not ministry which is the particular preserve and privilege of the ordained clergy) which Morton and Russell call for? How can we prepare for that new ministry in our theological seminaries, our church assemblies, our local parishes and congregations? Is such new ministry even possible, or will Scripture and the Tradition of the Church always constitute, in Stendahl's words, "an ever-available force toward the perpetuated bondage of women in subordination"? Does this mean that if women remain in the church, we are doomed forever to the following hierarchical order, suggested by Morton:

GOD

MAN

WOMAN

CHILD

EARTH

Intimately and inescapably related to the issue of new forms of ministry is the matter of new formulations of theology and new expressions of liturgy. What can best assist us in our attempts to comprehend, articulate, and celebrate our lives as full human beings—aid us in our worshipping, questioning, and witnessing? Can ritual and imagery within the churches be used, not to keep us in our place but to expand the options opened to us in our imagination and in our reality? To create these new options will mean developing both new words *and* new practices. As Harrison points out, we must have "a full ministry aimed at finding ways to embody, communally, the meaning of the Christian gospel"; only then will we be able "to make that gospel *publicly comprehensible once again.*"

A third area involved in a consideration of women and ministry is the significance of women's entry into public and powerful roles in the liberal churches at a point in time when these denominations are in decline in membership and wealth. What does this influx of women—into the ordained ministry in particular; into a profession which has been (as Harrison points out) essentially "feminine" and nurturing in its assigned roles; into the servant function (as spelled out by Russell)—imply? Does the entry of women into professional positions in fact symbolize the further decline of the ministry as a profession and the Church as an institution? Russell mentions the shrinking job opportunities in the churches for everyone—male and female—at this juncture.[3] If there will be only the remnant of an institution left to work in, then the question is raised, does it any longer matter whether or not a welcome is extended to women as full participants, ordained and/or lay?

Although Morton, Stendahl, and Harrison all touch upon the effects on men of the women's movement within the churches, much more thorough theoretical and clinical work remains to be done on this subject. What psychic threat do men who have filled essentially "feminine" roles for years feel as women begin to work beside them as their titular equals? What are the best ways for them to recognize, integrate and overcome their anxieties? What changes are implied in the roles played by the clergy? Will it be possible for women and men ever to function together in ministry as equals, whether or not ordained, during this century?

And finally, can the Christian faith operate in the last quarter of the twentieth century as agent of liberation for women *and* men? Does it offer women spiritual and intellectual resources so that they can unashamedly derive satisfaction from work done outside the home? Can the anti-body bias of Christianity be overcome so as to enable women (and men as well) to experience and rejoice in the gift of their sensuality? Perhaps most centrally, are we within the churches capable of eliminating the familial images which crowd Scripture and liturgy—beginning with God the Father, and His earthly counterpart, the priest-father?

Women's Declaration of Independence

No more silence! Enough! say women in the churches. No more submission to the long patriarchal tradition nor to the authority of men *qua* men. We have begged and pleaded, and followed the rules, and have been conformist "soft feminists" for too long. Now you hear our cries of rage and disappointment; you hear our analysis of the whys of our past and the effect on our present.

But already we are beginning to leave all this behind us. Sexist religion is doomed in its sexism; if only because we women will no longer be complicit in our own oppression. No longer will we allow the analogy of creatures from another planet to be applied (and applicable) to us. We are responding to Morton's call to "unleash our imaginations," to Daly's invitation to the experience of "contagious freedom," and we are creating our own future. We will rejoice in our creation as full human beings. We will celebrate our lives in the Spirit. We will be servants of liberation —of our own, certainly; of that of others as well, if possible.

Can the "faith of our fathers" be transformed into the hope of the new humanity, a hope which can give sustenance to ourselves and to coming generations of women and men? Can we develop what Morton calls the "apocalyptic community," where roles will no longer be assigned on the basis of gender, but on the variety of (non-anatomically-determined) gifts? In Acts we read of the experience of believers who held everything in common, and who made a brief foray into the world of neither poor nor rich, female nor male. In fact, some biblical commentators suspect that the section in I Timothy cited at the beginning of this Introduction came in part as a reaction to the "liberal" practices of the original Christian community regarding women. Is that experience of co-humanity (of the end of both the lower class and the inferior caste) possible for women in the church today?

As women who have been shaped by the Judaeo-Christian tradition, either we will transform the sexist religion which has held us (our minds and souls and bodies) captive these many years or we will create new communities of women and men in which we can receive the gifts of that Spirit which cannot ultimately be constrained by any institution, and which blows where it wills. No longer will we be spoken into silence. We are being heard into speech, and into life in all its fullness—within the Church if possible, outside the Church if necessary.

NOTES

1. These include: Kathleen Bliss, *The Service and Status of Women in the Churches* (London: SCM Press, Ltd., 1952); Margaret Eleanor Thrall's *The Ordination of Women to the Priesthood* (London: SCM Press, Ltd., 1958); Madelaine Barot's *Cooperation of Men and Women in Society* (Geneva: World Council of Churches, 1964); and Francine Dumas' *Man and Woman: Similarity and Difference* (Geneva: World Council of Churches, published in English, 1966). There were also André Dumas' analysis in *Concerning the Ordination of Women* (Geneva: World Council of Churches, 1964) and Krister Stendahl's *The Bible and the Role of Women* (Philadelphia: Fortress Press, published in English, 1966).
2. Elsie Thomas Culver's *Women in the World of Religion* (Garden City, N.Y.: Doubleday) was published in 1967, followed by Mary Daly's *The Church and the Second Sex* (New York: Harper and Row) in 1968. Significant additions to the lists during 1973–74 have been Emily Hewitt and Susan Hiatt, *Women Priests: Yes or No?* (New York: Seabury), Mary Daly, *Beyond God the Father: Toward a Philosophy of Women's Liberation* (Boston: Beacon), and Rosemary Ruether, ed., *Images of Women in the Jewish and Christian Traditions* (New York: Simon and Schuster). For listings of general material available on women and the church, see *Women's Liberation and the Church* (Sarah Bentley Doely, ed., New York: Association Press, 1970) and the Summer 1972 issue of *Theological Education* for helpful bibliographical and resource guides.
3. One clear example of this decline is shown in figures of the General Assembly Report of the United Presbyterian Church for 1972. During that year membership in the denomination declined to approximately 2,900,000—the first time in decades that membership had fallen below 3 million—and the number of congregations shrank by 27 to a total of 8,786. During the same year, however, the number of ordained ministers increased by 175 to 13,692. Reported in *A.D. (Presbyterian Life Edition)*, July 1973, p. 32.

PREACHING THE WORD[1]

Nelle Morton

What image is evoked by this usually-perceived-as-masculine vocation being dealt with by a woman speaker? To what extent does this image affect the way you begin to listen to what I say, and once listening, to the way you hear? Are you able to get in touch at a feeling level with that which is stirring in you?

Just suppose for a few moments that it is like this in your entire seminary life . . . that it is the *usual* thing to hear a woman's voice . . . that a male professor in the classroom is the *exception*, the *interruption*! How do you begin to feel, if you are a man? How, if a woman?

Suppose not only the professors but the predominance of students are women . . . that Harvard has a history as a woman's institution, with a feminine operational style?

What is evoked in you as you gradually become aware that the language in such an institution has a distinctly feminine character . . . that feminine words function for both masculine and feminine . . . that every time a professor says *womankind* she means, of course, "all humanity"? When one enrolls in a seminar on "The Doctrine of Woman" the professor intends at least to deal with men also. When one sings of the Motherhood of God and the Sisterhood of Woman, one breathes a prayer that all men as well as women will come to experience true sisterhood.

Intellectually you know all the time what is meant and that this is the way it has been for generations. But what do you begin to know out of your gut?

How do you feel, if you are a man, when you have raised the

question about the generic usage and have been dismissed by women who insist it is merely a semantic form? How do you feel, if you are a woman, when the few men around keep hammering on the fact that they experience alienation by such language?

What kind of support do you feel (if you are a woman) or lack of support (if you are a man) when you realize that it is like this in the whole world and that it has been this way since you were a little boy or a little girl? That there has never been a male President of the United States . . . that all seminaries and most universities have women presidents and deans? It should come as no surprise to you that most seminarians are women, since the seminary's woman recruiter has no particular program to enroll men. It is understandable why all the men students should feel they are on trial —you know, having to prove themselves. Imagine the frustration when a man uses his energy to get a hearing and has little left for creativity!

Once in a while a man gets nerve enough to protest the use of Mother God, saying that it does something to his sense of dignity and integrity. Professor Martha hastens to explain that no one really believes that God is female in a sexual sense. She makes it quite clear that in a matriarchal society the wording of Scripture, of liturgy and theology, could only come out in matriarchal imagery. The last student who raised such a question, it was discovered later, had just joined a male liberation group and it had gotten him all screwed up. Everyone knows that this man came to the Divinity School in the first place to get married, and eventually to be able to keep house and support his woman in her pastorate. What images function here? How do they make you feel if you are a man? If you are a woman? What sense of self-worth or value of being human is raised?

Let us follow such a seminarian a step further. It soon becomes obvious that he is denying his masculinity, that he is forgetting his true vocation bestowed upon him by the Creator Herself. No one is wise enough to know why God made female reproductive organs compact and internal so that woman is physically free to move about unencumbered and take her natural place of leadership in the world of womankind. Or why God made the male's organs external and exposed, so that he would demand sheltering and protection from the outside in order that he may be kept for reproducing the race. Any time a male student rejects his own built-in longing to be enfolded by a woman, or to give his woman a female child, or to enhance her vocation, he is in trouble. He becomes a fit subject for the best female therapist the Divinity School can secure. Feel into this. Feel for all men in all divinity schools. Feel for women—that is, generically speaking, when one person begins to cut himself off from the community sisterhood by rejecting his own creation.

Needless to add, the young seminarian is led by the therapist back into his childhood where he is able to get in touch with his internalized envy of his sister who could run and dance and climb and ride horseback preparing herself for leadership. Finally he is able to deal with her long-remembered jeering at his organs, which she said "flopped foolishly."

As with most minority students no serious therapy is demanded. In an encounter group with a competent woman trainer and the help of two men and ten women he soon develops a better attitude toward his divinely destined role and looks forward to giving his future wife the support she needs to be a real woman in the world.[2]

In the same spirit, though without the fantasy—but, on second thought, maybe a bit of fantasy at that—let us seek to evoke some of the images surrounding the pulpit, the altar, and the baptismal font where the church claims the Word of God becomes most visible and most audible.

For hundreds of years an aura of holiness has been maintained about the altar, until today it has become the focus of the place of women in the church and symbolic of the church's male supremacy. Relaxation of male control has changed little except in form since 1825 when a Jonesboro, Tennessee, women's society was thanked for raising the enormous sum of $40.25 for missions:

> The lovely and retiring modesty of the female sex, together with their delicate structure, forbids that they shall ever rival the hardy sons of Levi in the gross services of the altar. The Kind Author of our being never designed them [to] . . . search of lost sinners. . . . And yet they may be abundantly useful; yea, they are greatly so. They not only welcome weary pilgrims to their friendly mansions and hospitable cottages but they warm, clothe and feed them. . . .[3]

In order to get at what was going on here and continues to go on in churches, it is necessary to remind ourselves that images function powerfully long after they have been repudiated intellectually. They may continue to function until dealt with at the only level where they can be altered—that is, in the community psyche. I shall seek to evoke some of these images rather than present an argument; to raise questions about them rather than suggest answers.

It is a matter of history that the majority of church bodies in America have one by one opened doors officially to women for ordination. Ordination grants the privilege of *preaching the word*. The Catholic Church, the Orthodox communions, the Episcopal, and the Missouri Lutheran denominations in barring women from the pulpit may have a greater self-understanding than the so-called open churches. Their official pronouncements, while discriminating against women, at least coincide with their practice. At the same time, it may be observed that no "open" church body includes more than a minuscule proportion of ordained women.

Women candidates in the open churches claim they are discouraged from entering the pulpit through subtle and devious methods. In the spring of 1973 a woman seminary graduate meeting initially with the district committee on ministry was given to understand that if she sought other than a parish ministry—i.e., a ministry in which she would not preach, baptize, marry, or bury—the committee would be more open to receiving her. Not one question was she asked that pertained to her commitment, her understanding of ministry, her theology, or her beliefs. They let her know that they considered her highest qualification lay in her being a wife and a mother. This same woman was featured in a film produced by her denomination. There was resistance at first to inclusion of a scene showing her in the pulpit on the ground that churches would be offended. But her faithful persistence led both to her ordination and the retention of the pulpit scene. Three years ago another woman graduate of the same seminary, finding it difficult to get ordained in her state, applied to a neighboring one. In an initial interview the pastor of a well-known church opened conversation with her by asking: "How do you handle your sex life?"

In January 1973 I was invited to meet with a group of ministers. I found myself in the presence of angry and puzzled women, all beautiful, competent, and theologically able. They had been moved frequently by the official hierarchy. Some had been sent to remote areas. Some had not been received fully in church courts and church dialogue. A few were on the verge of opting out of the church completely. Some serving in joint pastorates with their husbands reported ministerial committees who viewed skeptically a husband in such an open relationship of mutuality.

The question emerges out of the reality of these and numerous other situations: What is it about the Word of God that makes it so important for the proclaimer of that Word to be of a certain sex, and that sex male?

Why is it that even when they are robed or gowned, clergymen breaking bread and pouring wine manage to project an image of the authority of maleness, with no suggestion of femaleness?

How is it that the Word of God has become identified with a deep voice? Is God dependent on sex?

What kind of theology is it that requires male hands for a sacrament to have efficacy?

Everywhere women ministers witness that they experience resistance to, and fear of, their ministry, not from the local churches but from ministers who ordain them and from whom they must receive approval on their way to a parish. One is forced to question the quality of education these men have received in theological schools that contributes to such continued discrimination. Could it be that theological schools have overlooked the male imagery they have perpetuated in theology, church history and liturgy, preaching, teaching and pastoring—not to mention male structure and model of the male professor! Could it be that they have concentrated on conceptual to the exclusion of holistic learning? In what seminary have myth, image, and symbol received more than a cerebral nod? Perhaps modern man, and I do not use that term generically, thinks he is beyond myth!

Have theological professors been unaware of the power of images and the way they concretize themselves sociologically, shaping community and individual life-styles long before persons conceptualize? Or do they not know how sociological structures may manufacture or evoke a myth or image to support and harden the structure? Years ago it was observed how an interchangeable use of images for *black* such as "dark," "sin," "dirty," "foreboding," "ugly"; and for *white* such as "pure," "sinless," "clean," "light," "truth," tended to produce an inferior self-image in black children and a superior self-image in white children before either arrived at the age of conceptualization. Dr. John Money makes a more startling observation from his clinical findings. The sex identity of a child, he says, is established by the time a child is eighteen months old. By the age of three sex identity is set as hard as concrete, so powerfully have the cultural images done their work. It is more difficult, states Dr. Money, to change even so early a mistaken identity than it is to stimulate by physical operation sex organs corresponding to the mistaken identity.[4]

But the question persists: Why has preaching the Word become the crux of the place of women in the life of the church?

I believe that women preaching, more than any aspect of the church's ministry, threatens to expose the church and its seminaries as primarily masculine institutions rather than human communities.

Consider what might happen with women in the holy places: behind the pulpit, proclaiming the Word, breaking the bread, consecrating the elements, baptizing, burying, and marrying!

By her very presence a woman would confront the church daily with its own baptism. As preacher she might serve as a catalyst for unleashing the imagination of the people for all kinds of creative lay ministries, new styles of relatedness, of being present to one another, gifts of grace to one another. The entire laity just might come to know itself as ministry—a people of God in the world in the truest and most radical sense. The new language and the new speech emerging out of such common involvement in ministry, listening, and living might furnish a new kind of movement and song for celebration. And then celebration itself could indeed become the work of the people, rising out of the heart of a people rather than structured and controlled from above.

Once the pulpit is de-sexed it can no longer be labeled as the phallic symbol in the sanctuary with the Book on top to give it authority. Women would more than likely carry the Book down among the people, open it, saying, "See . . . see for yourselves! Read! How do you read? See . . . see, even here seeds of liberation long ago overlooked by a patriarchal mind-set and culture." Then the most ignorant ones and timid might obtain courage to open their eyes and self-confidence to begin to think for themselves theologically. Should that happen, most embarrassing questions would inevitably be raised . . . agonies and lostnesses . . . alienations and oppressions . . . would be articulated unashamedly and boldly. In time an entire people might come to know itself as disinherited and open itself for the liberating experience of a new humanity.

Such a movement would inevitably bring to death a certain ecclesiastical hierarchy in allowing women—that is, those who wear the skirts all the time—to enter the pulpit in any great number to preach the Word.

By the same token, breaking bread and pouring wine—once seen as the serving role in which women are cast all the time—might reduce the holiness of the altar. Why should eating of the bread and drinking of the wine be separated from the consumption of the kindly fruits of the earth? Are not both simple acts of faith? Should not all that one eats be valued both physically and spiritually? Is it not time to rescue the powerful symbolism surrounding the sacrament from a preoccupation with things, and restore it to eating and drinking out of the people's common humanness at the deepest sources of their existence, where the bread and the wine lead out to the boundary of a new future?

Were women allowed to baptize openly, the uterine waters of baptism might begin to heal the split between physical birth and spiritual birth, since both are ejections out of the Great Womb. It might even herald the end of "joining a church." More realistically, the newly-born would be engrafted into a community of faith—received into its deaths, its births, its life, its struggles, and its joys in the world—sustained by a grace not conditioned by sex. The community of faith would embrace the totality of life's experiences in which God is not absent from any. There would be no point to postponing the new birth ritual to a time when the mind could begin to grasp its mysteries. Inevitably, new birth would shift to that moment from which it was once split off by a patriarchal perception which assigned body to woman and spirit to man. It would affirm that persons are loved before they comprehend, are in the struggle before they choose to be. Indeed it would envision a love that enables understanding; that begets trust; that calls persons to pick up their own lives as sacred gifts, not leaving them to the mercy and pressures of stereotyped images that rob them of their humanness.

What would happen to adults in churches—or to churches themselves, for that matter—if women ministers should receive children as "in ministry," and not objects "to be ministered to"? Undoubtedly Jesus placed a child in the inner midst of his disciples neither as an object lesson nor essentially for the sake of the child, but to confront the entire community with its own faith because the child belongs in ministry. Has the child not been relegated to a place of insignificance in the church to avoid reminding adults of too much unfinished business in their own lives? Is not the child in touch with resources that adults no longer value or have lost the ability to value or even to understand? Removing a child from the church's core ministry simply robs the church of its own faith and reduces its celebrative life to a blandness devoid of the ecstatic and the mysterious. Baptism, no matter at what age, serves as the symbolic act by which a community engrafts a person in ministry. As baptism is one baptism so ministry is one ministry. Therefore, to identify ministry "to children," rather than "children in ministry," becomes another betrayal of the community's faith. It would be a strange phenomenon, indeed, should the church and not the world begin to usher in the next and perhaps the final liberation movement—that of children.

The imagery in male language and structure serves to alienate women and dehumanize men.

Once the alienating male language and imagery in liturgy become inappropriate, it might be possible to celebrate out of the common life of a people rather than out of a superstructure manipulated from above that can only come through as phony to the oppressed. But women do not want the celebrative life of the community to be feminine any more than they want it to continue masculine. There is no objection to theologizing out of masculine experience. The basic problem lies in claiming the resulting theology valid for the entire community. Distortion occurs when the part parades for the whole.

Women shun a monopoly on the community's symbolic acts. They do not seek a feminine theology except iconoclastically to show up one kind of idolatry with another. All they want is the elimination of sexism at the core of the church and seminary life so that a new kind of transcendence may be experienced in the human flesh. It was none other than that male chauvinist Luther who said: "The deeper we can fetch Christ into the flesh the better it is for us all."

Given the partisan state of the church, women have hesitated to take those positions of leadership that have been open to them. In the first place, they have been conditioned all their life not to seek positions of authority; and many who seek such positions are preconditioned to fail even when they have the ability to succeed. Many women are unable to take on the "man's way" without losing their integrity. They feel that the present male structure and tight male control allow for little flexibility. Women experience dehumanization in seminaries and churches by inequity of salaries, promotion, rank, and limited dialogical participation. Women hesitate to recommend one another at a first vacancy in a seminary or church, or to become aggressive themselves in seeking churches and the ministry, teaching and administrative positions. They feel that by and large men still want token women. And tokenness is no step at all to freedom. Women are convinced that once they are heard and received, a new and as yet unknown way that transcends sexism will emerge. But women are fast losing hope that hearing will or can take place.

The males in control in both seminaries and church courts find it difficult or nearly impossible to hear the preached Word as Word from a woman's lips because of the imagery operating in their own life which identifies a woman by her sex function.

The *Windham Journal* report of Maggie Van Cott's appearance in the Hudson Street Methodist Church pulpit in 1869 and brief vignettes following indicate how imagery functions so as to screen a woman's words and message.

> The clerical toilet of the Rev. Widow Van Cott, as she stood up before the multitude . . . and dispensed the Word, is described as having been neat, and that she looked as blooming and blushing as a newly-made bride. Her hair was nicely fixed and frizzed, and her face glowed with a modest but conscious splendor, as she stood before the congregation in her rich but tasteful dress of bombazine. She wore a neat black jet ornament on her throat, and a handsome gold chain peeped from the black belt around her waist. Every word she uttered was delivered with unction and force. There is considerable power and

attraction in the manner in which the widow lifts her smooth white hand and nicely rounded fingers to the ceiling, and then brings them down with energy on the wooden shelf of the pulpit. When warmed to her subject her face seems lighted up and full of stirring animation. Her face in happy moments contracts and expands, and her handsomely shaped body sways to and fro with excitement. Her elocution is natural and florid, and her sentences uttered in a bass tone voice.[5]

A century later *The New York Times* reported the occasion on which a woman in a certain New York church first preached under a prominent caption: "A Grandma Preaches at Riverside."[6]

When a small New Jersey church ordained its first woman minister some of her ministerial colleagues referred to her as "the preacher who wears skirts," except in small intimate circles, where they said, "The new preacher does not wear pants."

"Balloonist's Widow, 77, Joins Seminary to Pursue Long Ambition—Priesthood," said the announcement of Mme. Piccard's enrollment in theological school in the fall of 1972.[7] The same issue of the newspaper headlined the story of another woman pictured with a group of ministers: "Grandmother's Path to Pulpit Is Long."[8]

A woman was recommended for an Old Testament post in a leading seminary. Her qualifications were excellent. The student committee was enthusiastically for her appointment. The Old Testament professors wanted her. After lengthy discussion of her in a faculty meeting one member pushed his chair back from the table and announced emphatically: "She just doesn't turn me on." The woman was not offered the position.

Identifying and describing any person in the pulpit or classroom by their sex function is immoral.

To summarize: women such as those mentioned above experience a great sense of alienation by this kind of immorality reflected in generic language, in male imagery, in hierarchical structures. But they confess the ultimate alienation lies in the persistent and pervasive masculine character and control of the institution, the ontological maleness of Transcendence with its theological spinoff out of the male rather than out of the full human experience.

While women are constantly up against the limitations of language to express full humanity we have now available a more adequate language than we are willing to use. Consider how much richer one's speech is in the use of *humankind* rather than *mankind* and *all persons* instead of *all men.*

A fundamental question now insinuates itself: Could the limiting imagery in the word Word—"logos"—derive from a patriarchal way of perceiving and experiencing the universe? Would a more inclusive perceiving allow for persons to be heard into existence rather than spoken into existence?

Could it be that *Logos* deified reduces communication to a one-way relationship—that of *speak*-ing—and bypasses the far more radical divine aspect of *hearing*?

Once such a possibility is entertained, and the biblical confession read from that perspective, is not one confronted by a pervasive Wisdom in the universe which *Logos* and its self-extension *technology,* seek to manipulate and control? That the more divine act is *hearing to speech* rather than *speaking to speech*? That the pervasive Wisdom or Transcendent One hears the human being to speech; and that the word is the human being's word; and that word heard into speech creates and announces new personhood—new consciousness awakened in the human being.

Every liberation movement rises out of its bondage with a new speech on its lips. This has been so with women coming together, seeking to get in touch with their own stories and experiences which they have discovered welling up from within, from underneath, from out of their past, from out of their traditions rather than down from above. But to evoke her story to speech woman experiences an imperative—a prior great Listening Ear . . . an ear which hears her without interruption down through her defenses, clichéd language, pretensions, evasions, pervasive hurts, angers, frustrations, internalized stereotyped images until she experiences at the lowest point of her life that she is sustained. Women are literally hearing one another to speech. But the speech is their speech. It may come on stumblingly or boldly. But it is authentically themselves.

Through hearing and speaking, women sense the possibility of theologizing out of their own experiences. They better understand how church dogmas, ecclesiastical practices, liturgies, and language that are oppressive of and exclude women have derived from male experience. Only a masculine hierarchical scale of values could project the imagery in order of decreasing value of:

GOD
MAN
WOMAN
CHILD
EARTH

Such a hierarchical system, leaving no room for the human, could have toppled long ago had the so-called recipients of the revelation been sensitive to that which happened in their midst and allowed themselves to be heard into a new radical liberating speech.

Let us examine briefly the system out of which theologizing has taken place for more than two thousand years. Only the child ranked beneath the woman in first-century Palestinian culture. But the girl-child was considered of infinitely less value than the boy-child. The only human creature lower than the girl-child was the boy-child who had no father, who had no name, who had no lineage—an illegitimate one, a bastard. The dictionary terms such a one "inferior to or varying from standard." An illegitimate girl, as viewed by a patriarchal society, could marry into a name. A bastard boy—never! In such a one—lower than the lowest, cut off out of the land of the living—could the most lost or oppressed of the earth find himself or herself . . . God-with-us . . . Emmanuel. But a patriarchy could not bear so radical a salvation. Rather than permit the hierarchy to falter they quickly snatched the child out of his low estate and set him up at the right hand of the Father—thus shoring up the old ontological masculinity of God, interpreting the event with such a theological superstructure as to institutionalize its maleness with built-in protection against women and children. So it has continued to this day—due largely to the powerful functioning of imagery and ritual.

Seminaries keep supplying churches with ministers and universities with religion professors who have never come to terms with the way images go underground, shape life-styles, and set a kind of mentality that is no longer able to perceive wholeness.

The woman movement confronts the churches and seminaries with an opportunity to respond in terms of the deepest cleavage in the human experience—that of sex. It cannot be turned off or easily dismissed. Its ferment is stirring in countries around the world, countries unrelated to one another—like mushrooms springing up out of the darkness. It carries a cosmic overtone. The word of Betty Friedan in 1963 and Simone de Beauvoir twenty years earlier and the feminists of the last century did not start the movement. These women merely gave public utterance to the private whisperings that have been heard into expression for generations. Today the movement accelerates as a massive shifting of perceived reality and, in the words of theologian Mary Daly, "a vast reordering of the forces of the universe."[9] A biblical writer could well have envisioned such a moment:

> We know that the whole creation has been groaning in travail together until now; and not only the creation, but we ourselves . . . (Rom. 8:22–23)

Thus we are brought near to the possibility of new revelatory moments that break into the present and open a hopeful future for all humanity.

In the light of all this, what could the churches' renewed emphasis on evangelism possibly mean to women at this moment in their history?

What hope does it offer to those women who are already on the rolls of the institutions or, for that matter, to those who are outside—to that more than half of the human race—the subjugated half!

Of the nearly one hundred on the planning committee of Key '73, an interdenominational cooperative evangelistic effort, I was told by an official that only one woman was included.

A national television series interpreting this new thrust engaged in dialogue each Sunday morning a group of two or three men, in addition to the moderator. The language of the dialogue, out of the male experience, came through to me and many other women as a foreign language:

Jesus Christ as the Word for modern *man*
He is the Word for all *men*
As *men* hear the gospel . . .
As *men* communicate the gospel
Calling *men* to repentance and renewal of life,

difficult in our culture . . . but still good news to *men*
Good news to poor *men* . . . liberation to bound *men*
Men need what the church has to give

One minister ventured: "But if news is good to the poor . . . liberation for the oppressed . . . it may be bad news to the top dogs." He was not heard, even though he repeated his remark.

In no plans that I have seen or heard has the current brand of evangelism promised to herald the end of sexism and usher in a new human community in which all persons could receive the gift of their uniqueness, stand up, and be responsible because they are so enabled by the inclusiveness of community which ever examines itself in light of its confessed faith. Therefore I do not see local churches, as the TV panel indicated, nor the ghettoes as the new missions fields today, but the seminaries and the ministers they produce. For it is they who continue to proclaim a Word which comes through as a male word from a male god.

Ecclesiastical institutions continue to operate out of a prophetic rather than out of an apocalyptic model. The prophetic relies on the expert, the insightful and powerful leaders, the stars and the superstars who read the signs of the times, pronounce the word of the hour, and command obedient but individualistic followers. Since the prophetic model depends on a hierarchical ordering of values its best expression can never fully transcend the status quo. The apocalyptic, on the other hand, takes with dead seriousness the reality of community, recognizing the infinite and unique value of the "least one" within it. It cannot afford to listen only to the expert and the star. It relies more on faithfulness in the humanizing and politicizing process. Its ear is tuned to transcendence at the heart of the body politic, thus allowing for a totally new break-in that cannot be predetermined or manipulated or controlled by any one mind. Since the apocalyptic hopes for a new humanity, the dynamic of its daily life contributes to its actualization.

What this implies for theological curricular development and for the church's ministry in terms of method, content, and structure is unlimited. Many seminaries are still under the illusion that the involvement/reflection model has eliminated the old dichotomy between theory and practice, when as a matter of fact it has merely reordered the pieces.

Liberation derives not from individuation *per se* but from the humanness of an authentic community in which identity can be defined in terms of person and not in terms of anatomy or grade. Self-actualization becomes a misleading term when thought of only as "forever moving toward one's full potential." I am speaking of a liberation that emerges out of one's true beginning . . . one's deepest roots.

"Humanizing the hierarchical structures in churches" is one stated goal of the newly established Commission on the Status and Role of Women in the United Methodist Church. Many church women support their effort, but just as many are beginning to take a dim view as to whether the church can be saved—or will change. "The coming of woman will be the final humanization of the species," wrote Betty Farians when she was chairwoman of NOW's (National Organization of Women) National Task Force on Religion.[10]

Many women have gotten their first glimmer of liberation in the community of faith. They say that in spite of the male control something came through to them, for they do not believe God is intimidated by maleness. But they are now coming to see that that which came to them was not what the church was saying . . . not what men in the pulpit are saying today, or mean. Women are hearing in the churches not a word which liberates, but language which alienates, which drives them to one another, and to the Spirit of all which has enabled them to survive and which literally brought them from death to life.

Women, as indicated earlier, are not concerned to open up churches and seminaries in order that more women be received into a sexist order. But women are concerned to be heard. They believe that once men begin to hear—can hear, really hear and see—a new order and a new language free from sexism could emerge.

By her conditioned nature woman finds it hard to rebel—even from a sexist institution of which she is the victim. She has been led to believe that rebellion violates her femininity. Yet there may come a time, and soon, when rebellion becomes her only positive response to that Great Source of life with which she is now in touch and from which she receives nourishment. When the chips are down and women have to choose between that which heard them to speech and the hierarchical voices that maintain control they have no choice, for they know they are in touch with the life sources of their humanness. Women are not about to let go that which has brought them to life. And all over, women are experiencing God as a great hearing one, one who heard them to speech, rather than one who has spoken them to hearing.

It may be that which a more patriarchal-minded critic has condemned in Ingmar Bergman as the silence of God (in which God is perceived as inept and people perceived as hopelessly facing the meaninglessness and absurdity of life) may be near to the woman's experience of God as *hearing her to speech*. Freed from the authoritarian hang-up, it is in that moment in every Bergman film that human communication at its deepest level becomes the most crucial part of the film. Otherwise the communicator is dead. And it is in that moment that love looms as a most poignant reality.

A stronger metaphor for loving than "touch" or "word," Bergman asserts in his film *Cries and Whispers,* is that guttural cry out of the extremity of one's existence. As one becomes aware early in the film that the deepest pain is dying in life and not dying in death, one expects the cries of Agnes, one of the three sisters, to be primarily physical pain from her terminal cancer. Maria, a second sister, cries out at Agnes' clinging corpse which confronts her with her own death—with the end of her constant touching and using of others. Her dismissal of the faithful service of Anna with the afterthought of a bill thrust into her hand becomes the final symbol of her shallowness. Only Karin, the third sister, is left. Karin, the stern, tall, beautiful, tender one hidden beneath layer after layer of stiff, corseted brocade. Only Karin backs up against the wall and cries out from the bowels of her earth. Only Karin has courage to lacerate her own body as primordial witness to an already dead marriage relationship. Only Karin rebuffs Maria with "Don't touch me" . . . "Don't touch me" . . . "Don't touch me," as she senses the sister's touch possessive and not loving.

Authentic speech begins with the guttural cry at the extremity of one's own self-seeking, one's well-ordered, stereotyped life. It informs the film of the ineffectuality of ordinary communicative techniques, of mechanical devices that attempt to tick off and control time. It confesses the limits of contrived groups, encounters, and instruments that claim health and intimacy when there is only triteness and counterfeit. A guttural cry in one brief moment marks the end of the phony and reverses the ordinary.

And in that reversal the self is freed from its boundness and participates in a transcendent spiritual identification with others appropriating a kind of grace that enables praise.

It is in this sense that we celebrate the Eucharist, in which the Risen One becomes present in the common meal. "The cult is regarded almost as an anticipation of the Messianic event,"[11] in which Christ comes present and the fellowship of the participants becomes alive and *radical.* Here is evoked the most ancient and primitive Christian liturgy. Cullmann says it goes back to the Didache and started in an ancient Egyptian liturgy. It does *not* contain the Words of Institution or reference to the death of Christ.

Celebration can also be traced through the Latin *celebratus,* a past participle of *celebrare,* which literally means "to observe frequently, to commemorate, to honor or praise publicly." In that sense the ancient liturgy of St. Hyppolytus is evoked which is dominated by the idea of the death of Christ and inspired by the Words of Institution. It thus becomes more a commemoration of an event that has happened rather than a new creation in the relationship of the people.

In that spirit, the new woman can no longer buy the structured-from-above celebrative techniques. They come to her as manipulative and phony. With her sisters she knows celebration as out of the depths, out of the silent hollow darkness. Up from the roots. Thus we redeem the history of the word, looking to the Greek rather than to the Latin for its origins. *Cele* or *coele,* meaning "cavity, emptiness, hollow," with *brata,* "to rule, command," becomes "to command the emptiness," to fill the void with that which by nature alone one does not possess.

Praise, then, for the new woman comes out of a reality before the actuality . . . before the fact . . . before the word she cannot yet speak. A great hearing shapes her guttural cry into a

HALLELUJAH!

because she *is*

and *is alive.*

NOTES

1. This topic was not of my choosing, but was assigned to me by those who organized this lecture series.
2. The idea for this experiment came from Theo Wells, "Woman—Which Includes Man, of Course: An Experience in Awareness," *Newsletter for Humanistic Psychology* (San Francisco), December 1970.
3. Mabel K. Howell, *Women and the Kingdom: Fifty Years of Kingdom Building by Women of the Methodist Episcopal Church South, 1878–1928* (Nashville: Cokesbury, 1928), pp. 24–25.
4. John Money and Anke A. Ehrhardt, *Man and Woman: Boy and Girl—Differentiation and Dimorphism of Gender Identity* (Baltimore: Johns Hopkins University Press, 1972), pp. 12–16, and Chapter 7.
5. Elaine Magalis, *Conduct Becoming to a Woman* (New York: Women's Division/Board of Global Ministries/The United Methodist Church, 1973), pp. 112–113.
6. *New York Times,* May 18, 1968.
7. *Ibid.*, October 1, 1972.
8. *Ibid.*
9. From a conversation.
10. Quoted from paper "The Coming of Woman," copyright Betty Farians, April 1971.
11. Oscar Cullmann, and Franz J. Leenhardt, *Essays on the Lord's Supper*. Ecumenical Studies in Worship, No. 1 (Richmond: John Knox Press, 1958), p. 14.

WOMEN AND MINISTRY

Letty M. Russell

The Problem of Ministry

The understanding and practice of ministry has been a problem in the life of Christian churches for some time. Changes in the structure of society and the church have brought with them ever-changing roles. Identity crises are common among clergy of all confessions as they try to reinterpret their calling in the light of personal and ecclesial needs. Personal and institutional financial crises result in personal insecurity and anxiety as job openings become less available.

Such problems are compounded for women engaged in ministry. As more and more women seek an education that will prepare them for clerical ordination, the old roles of male clergy appear even more restrictive and inadequate. Pressure on the job market by women, who are beginning to constitute as much as 30 per cent of theological seminary enrollment, is a threat not only to churches who refuse to ordain women, but also to those churches who have no job openings for them when they graduate.

These problems are further compounded by the anachronistic understanding of clerical ordination which exists, in practice if not in theory, in all churches which continue to be male-dominated on the local, national, and international levels. Pressure for the liberation of women in societies around the world is slowly exposing the sexist practices of church life, language, and organization. A persistent chorus of voices, both female and male, is calling for a new look at the meaning of ministry and mission in a world crying out for justice and liberation for all peoples.

On the surface it does not seem difficult to describe the meaning of ministry. *Ministry* comes from the Greek word *diakonia* and means "service." In its most simple form, ministry is following the One who came "not to be served but to serve" (Matt. 20:28).

Yet the word *ministry* (*diakonia*) immediately raises at least two problems for women who wish to serve in and through the contemporary church. First, ministry is identified in our minds with the word *minister* or *priest* and, therefore, with an all-male caste system which dominates the work of most churches. Second, women, like other oppressed groups, resent being identified with a role of servant which has long been a symbol of their oppression in family, church, and society. It is simply *not* Good News to someone trying to break out of the "servant class" to hear that God has called her to be a servant!

These two pressing problems confront women as they consider the theory and practice of ministry. Therefore, it is important to explore the problem of minister and of servant in the light of the changing roles of women in the church today.[1]

The Ministry as a Male Caste

The identification of the word *minister* with a certain status or class symbolized by clerical ordination raises many questions for both women and men considering ordination or service in a variety of church ministries. For many people this form of status seems dysfunctional in the modern, more democratic structures of society.

Minimal ecumenical consensus. The question of clerical ordination has been widely investigated in the last twenty years in every theological discipline as well as in related social sciences.[2] A minimal ecumenical consensus seems to have been reached on certain points which do not have much actual effect on ordination practices.

There is agreement that the ministries of the church are derivative from Christ in his threefold function of Prophet, Priest, and King. This is known in theological writings as the *triplex munus.*[3] There is also agreement that this ministry is the calling of the whole people of God although only certain people are set aside by clerical ordination.[4] Lastly there is agreement that the New Testament reflects a varied pattern of ministry: including that of bishop and deacon in the Pauline churches which recognized a wide variety of *charismata* but no ordination, and that of presbyter in the Palestinian churches which did practice ordination.[5]

This generalized consensus immediately breaks down in the varieties of theological and nontheological factors which shape the traditions of ordination in the various confessions. Therefore, it is of minimal use when women and men set out to change constitutional, canonical, and ecclesiastical practices which separate churches in matters of recognition of orders, intercommunion, and the ordination of women.[6]

Identity crisis in the church. The particular patterns of clerical ordination in the church confessions are historically conditioned and are derived from particular understandings of the church. At the present time there seems to be no clear understanding of the way in which the church should carry out God's Mission in a pluriform society. This confusion both of vision and tactics results in an identity crisis in ecclesiastical organization and ordination practices.

The traditional approaches to the meaning of clerical ordination are clearly reflective of particular ecclesial positions. Those who consider the priesthood to be of the *esse* (or "being") of the church and the representation of Christ in the church tend to suggest the restriction of ordination to the sacramental and pastoral role, possibly extending it to deacons or older men and to those without theological training in places of severe shortage as in the mission field. Those who consider ministry to be the *plene esse* ("necessary to the fullness of the church") or the *bene esse* ("necessary to the well-being of the church") tend to suggest broadening of ordination to many walks of life and to the so-called specialized ministries.[7] There are others, of course, who consider ministry in its present form to be the *male esse* ("bad for the life, renewal, and mission of the church") and tend to call for a new look at the way women and men are set aside for Christ's service.

Current positions and strategies among women. The positions of women on this matter are just as varied. The strategies which they use concerning the question of ordination for women depend on the tradition within which they are working and on the immediate problems faced.

Those who still face the *exclusion* of women from ordination are pushing hard to translate the theologians' consensus that nothing prevents it into a political consensus that women have no defect which bars them from sharing with men in the tasks of ministry (servanthood!). An excellent example of this, with ample presentation of the arguments for and against ordination, can be found in the book by Emily Hewitt and Suzanne Hiatt, *Women Priests, Yes or No?*[8] One of the problems of this position, which is avoided in the literature mentioned, appears to be that women have a tendency to buy into the clerical system rather than demanding transformation of the understanding of ministry so that men and women would have more creative roles to fulfill in the mission of the church. On the other hand, many women who may not wish to be ordained are often found among those who think that "it is the whole concept of priesthood which must be rethought."[9]

Those who face *de facto* exclusion of women from pastoral ministry as a result of lack of jobs for women who have been ordained are working on task forces, commissions, and committees, such as those in the United Church of Christ, the United Methodist Church, and the United Presbyterian Church in the U.S.A., which seek to enforce equal hiring practices at all levels of church life. Difficulties in this area are presented by the contracting job market in the church which increases the hostility of male clergy and slows down the process of change. In these situations women sometimes also face the opposition of volunteer women who do not yet see the importance of shared power and responsibility at every level of church life.[10]

Some women have long since grown disillusioned with the whole system of ordination as it is now practiced. They consider it to be dysfunctional and are pushing for new understanding of pluralized ministries of shorter duration which could include people from all walks of life. These women tend to see clerical ordination itself as a male caste system which must be transformed in order for non-whites and non-males to receive equal recognition and use of their gifts of the Spirit. The problem here is that such a change would mean radical renewal of the structures of church life at a time when the mood of the church seems to be one of retreat and consolidation.[11]

There is also a growing number of women who have simply decided to drop out of the organized church structures altogether.

They tend to look for alternative forms of community which allow sisterhood to flower without the restraints of male-dominated bureaucracies.[12] Women who take this position help to create breathing space for their sisters working within the organized church by their more radical stance from the outside. However, their position also presents problems arising from loss of a power base within the church. They leave to others the work of raising the consciousness of the vast majority of women who are church members and do have the power of numbers to transform the church for its mission in the world.

Having looked at the varieties of positions available to women at the moment in working for changes in the understanding of clerical ordination, it is important to remember that such a typology is only for the sake of analysis and understanding. In real life women find themselves in two or three categories at once, depending on the particular issue or moment in their own life. Yet one thing is clear: there is a growing number of women who are concerned about the ministry of the church and ways in which it can more fully represent a partnership of men and women in service.

Subverting the Clergy Line

While recognizing that all types of effort are crucial in the struggle of women against sexism in the church, my own position is that of the third category. I am trying to find ways of standing firmly within the organized church and of subverting what J. A. T. Robinson calls the "clergy line" in his book *The New Reformation?*[13]

I am interested in focusing on the ministry as the one calling (*klesis*) of Jesus Christ to all Christians which is expressed through baptism and commissioning to the use of particular *charismata* for the building up of the congregation in its service and mission in the world. A discussion of the theological background of this position has been published in an excellent booklet of the United Presbyterian Church in the U.S.A. called *Model for Ministry*.[14] The fact that the findings of that study were rejected by the General Assembly of that church in 1973 is indicative of how difficult it is to challenge the entrenched structures of privilege which now surround the clergy.

Dysfunctional sociological pattern. The traditional pattern of ordination as a means of confirming clerical status is becoming dysfunctional for the church. A line between clergy and laity tends to perpetuate a hierarchical system which places severe limitations on the relevance of the church to modern society and the ability of the church to serve where it is needed in that society.

The pattern as it exists today was developed out of Roman legal terminology to signify a certain status in the period of Christendom. This pattern is becoming very difficult to maintain in the modern period of voluntary, flexible organizations, and entrance into such a caste makes it very difficult for men and women to function in relevant ministry. The pattern was developed for use in the old parish system of the Middle Ages, and no amount of updating seems adequate to fit it for the variety of ministries needed in modern society.[15] Such a pattern of clerical status inhibits the possibility of participatory democracy and service on the part of the whole people of God. It continues to subvert the role of the laity and to exclude large groups of women and Third World people from full participation.[16]

Dysfunctional theological pattern. The patterns of clerical ordination have developed in the various traditions of the churches. There is no one pattern of ordination to be found in the New Testament except that of *diakonia.*[17] The early church viewed ministry simply as *diakonia* (service) and used the word in reference to function and not to status. The only essential ministry in the church was Christ's, and the variety of other forms was dependent on Christ and the Holy Spirit.[18]

The reformers of the sixteenth century also recognized the functional character of the ministry. The doctrine of the priesthood of all believers was extended by Luther and other reformers to the concept of vocation (*vocatio*), which before that time had been reserved for those who received a call to monastic life, to all the various stations in society. Just as all people were justified by faith, all people received a special call or vocation to the service of God. Because of the medieval social context, emphasis was soon placed on remaining in one's *station* in life so that the insight into universal *calling* was lost in the struggle to preserve rigid social structures or castes, including that of clergy.[19]

In our time the discussion among church confessions concerning their various traditions of ordination usually reaches a dead end. The position of each group is determined by the particular traditions of that group and its ideological formulation concerning its identity. As indicated above, the consensus usually goes no further than agreement on the threefold ministry of Christ, which belongs to the whole people of God. Perhaps it is time to begin again with some New Testament clues and the modern pluralistic context, and to refuse to continue to wait until some form of "faith and order" agreement can be reached which would bring all confessions together on these matters. One such new approach might be to begin with the meaning and function of God's mission as the key to ministries, rather than beginning with the traditions of ministry.[20]

If we begin with God's mission in handing over Jesus Christ into the hands of men and women of every land and generation, we are led to emphasize this traditioning activity (*paradosis*, Rom. 8:31–32) of God rather than the individual church traditions. The only true minister needful for that traditioning process is Jesus Christ through the Holy Spirit. The ministry of the church is to serve Christ's ministry of service in the world in whatever way is most helpful to the opening up of the future of humankind, and the sharing in the tasks of God's New Creation. Where a particular tradition of ordination is helpful to mission let it continue, but where this tradition stands in the way of communicating the gospel in the modern world, the church should search out the ways in which the Spirit is leading to new forms of ministry and mission.

A misfit strategy. I see my own ordination and work as a pastor and theologian as one way to break down the clergy line because I simply don't fit in this old male club. I myself and other ordained women are frequently an embarrassment to the male church establishment. Many things have to change because of our presence such as the language of clergy address, "Fathers and Brethren," the life-styles of clergy, and the way in which women perceive theology and ministry from their own life experience. Those women who refuse ordination and choose to serve in other ways also help from the other side, by creating new experimental models for ministry within their own traditions.

The most important aspect of this "misfit strategy" is not which personal choice a woman makes in the exercise of her Christian vocation, but the integrity with which she works to enable herself and all people to find structures and life-styles which will enable them to render relevant service to the needs of humanity in the modern world. In this way women who refuse to fit too easily into the old structures of the church can participate in renewing it as an instrument of God's mission and service.

Servanthood and Subordination

No matter what our position on the relation of ministry to the clerical ordination of ministers, as women we are also confronted with the word *ministry (diakonia)* and its meaning of servanthood. As Christians we cannot avoid the word, in spite of its symbolic oppressive overtones. Service is clearly a central part of the Gospel message of liberation. We are set free for others and made more fully human just because of our servanthood, according to the Gospel. But the word *servant* in the Gospel does *not* mean that Christians of any race, sex, or class are condemned to inferiority by other oppressing groups.

An instrument of divine help. The idea of servant in both the Old and New Testaments never is an indication of inferiority or subordination. It is significantly used to refer to service as a form of divine help. In Genesis 2:20 reference is made to the creation of woman to be Adam's helper. The Hebrew word for *helper* which is used in this passage is *'ezer*. In English *helper* implies someone who is a servant or subordinate. Yet in the twenty other times this word *'ezer* appears in the Old Testament we find that sixteen times it refers not to a subordinate, but to a superior form of help and it never refers to subordination.[21] Frequently the word is used of God, who is "a very present help [*'ezrah*] in trouble" (Ps. 46:01). From this we can conclude with André Dumas in the World Council of Churches booklet "Concerning the Ordination of Women" that to be a helper is to be an instrument of divine help or assistance to one in need.[22]

A similar significance is attached to the idea of helper or servant in other Old Testament concepts as well. Israel is chosen by God. This privilege of God's choice is a privilege of election for service. Israel's mission is to be an instrument for making God's love known to all the nations. Thus Isaiah writes, "Behold my servant, whom I uphold, my chosen, in whom my soul delights; I have put my spirit upon him, he will bring forth justice to the nations" (42:1).[23]

Christ as the image of servant. Certainly the image of the Suffering Servant from Isaiah with which the New Testament identifies Christ is clearly related to the Messianic image of the bringer of the new age of deliverance and liberation (Matt. 12:15–21; Acts 3:13). In fulfillment of his task Christ showed himself to be a servant of others because he "emptied himself, taking the form of a servant [*doulos*, "slave"], being born in the likeness of men [*anthropoi*, "humans"] (Phil. 2:7)."[24] This service to others on behalf of God was not a form of subordination to other people, but rather a free offering of self and an acceptance of service and love in return (Luke 7:36–50; 8:1–3; 10:38–42).

Apostles and servants. The word *apostle* in Pauline texts carries the same implication of one who has been called to serve in the witness of the Gospel. For this reason Paul speaks of Phoebe, Apollos, and himself as *diakonos* (Rom. 1:1; 16:1–2; 1 Cor. 3:5). In fact he even calls himself a slave *(doulos)* of Christ because this indicates his role as a participant in God's liberating action with Christ (1 Cor. 9:19). In the New Testament and in church history, women have also been referred to not only as servants, but also as apostles (witnesses) of Christ.[25] The first witnesses of the Resurrection who ran to tell the Good News were women (Luke 24:1–2). Among others, Origen of Alexandria and Bernard of Clairvaux speak of these women as well as the Samaritan woman (John 4:29–30) as apostles. Mary Magdalene has even been called "the apostle of the apostles."[26]

Regardless of what the role of servant has come to mean in the history of the church and society, in the Bible it is clearly a role of privilege and responsibility to take part in God's work of service in the world. Women and men are called by God in Jesus Christ to be both servants and apostles.

Servanthood and Sisterhood

Diakonia is not only a part of the Gospel story of liberation, it is also an indication of what it means to become more fully human. For according to the example of Jesus, to be truly human is to live in love and service toward others and toward God. Yet the clarity of this idea in Scripture does not easily dispel the problems which the idea of servanthood presents for women today as they struggle against roles of subordination in church and society. Somehow learning to be pro-woman and to affirm sisterhood seems to imply the rejection of the servant image.

Rejection of powerlessness. Women, like other oppressed groups in modern society, reject the idea of servanthood because they see it as an expression of their own powerlessness. Too long they have actually been the servants of *men.* Social structures have dictated the subordinate roles which women were allowed to play, and the male hierarchies of the churches have claimed divine sanction for these roles. It is no wonder that some women are declaring as firmly as Saint Peter ever did, "We must obey God rather than men" (Acts 5:29). Even the word *service* itself has become so debased in its common usage today that men and women alike often think of it only as referring to Band-Aid-type assistance. They have begun to speak of "social action" and "change agents" to describe a concern for others which expresses itself in attempts to change power structures which oppress and deprive people of their human rights.

The predominantly white and male clergy have used their position of power in the life of the local church to reinforce an inferior servant role of all the laity, as well as religious orders. Although the *laos* in its original sense includes *all* the people of God without distinction between ordained and unordained, the present structures of church life place the unordained (of which the majority are women) in the position of providing support services for the clergy.[27] No matter how powerful a women's organization or religious order may become because of its service or dedication, it remains subject to the structural and canonical limitations of churches which are ultimately controlled by men.

This actual situation frequently hampers the type and quality of service which women are able to render in the mission of the church. One of the ways to begin to change this, however, is to refuse to accept this situation of powerlessness and to reclaim the true meaning of *diakonia* as the basis for partnership in the church. It is important to be clear that *diakonia* is in fact the basis of genuine ecclesial power and authority. This is why Gregory the First called himself "the Servant of the Servants." The only genuine form of power in the church is that of service. As Paul put it, service is the power of inner authority which comes to those who are willing to "put their bodies on the line" ("present your bodies as a living sacrifice," Rom. 12:1).

The opposite of *diakonia*, according to Hans Küng in *Why Priests?*, is domination and misuse of power. Or, to turn it around, the opposite of domination is service or liberation! Women's liberation is not seeking domination and misuse of power, because women know that they will not have moved society toward new humanity and liberation if they have simply replaced one oppressor with another.

Sisterhood on the way to servanthood. The process of overcoming false domination in the name of genuine service or liberation is a difficult one for women. It begins with the women who become aware of the false contradictions in their situation and risk taking action to change them. This journey toward liberation is described by Paulo Freire in *Pedagogy of the Oppressed* as a process of *conscientization*: learning to perceive the social, economic, and political contradictions in society and to work in community with others to transform the world and build a new society.[28]

In coming to new awareness women must first learn to reject the role of submission to men. Such submission is in fact an element of human sinfulness in which women refuse to accept their full created humanity as partners with men in the work of God's mission in the world (Gen. 1:26–28). The assumption that service equals subordination is a form of "naive consciousness."[29] Interpretations such as that of Karl Barth which assert that man and woman were created as co-human, yet that woman is always second in God's order of creation have to be challenged if we are to assert our full co-humanity.[30] We have to be clear with ourselves and our sisters around the world about the distinction between God's ordering of creation and cultural expressions of various human societies.

Women must first learn to be pro-woman, and to accept sisterhood as applying to themselves and all other women, before they can begin to have a genuine approach to service as reflecting the role of "divine helper." Once they learn to accept their own identity as women, and to work out their own life-styles, then they are also able to find new ways of cooperating with men in being God's servants on behalf of all humanity.

Ultimately this can lead us to be not only pro-woman, but also pro-human and to accept a genuine reciprocal relationship of service. Such a relationship would be modeled on the life-style of Jesus so that women are set free both to serve and to be served without loss of identity and fear of subordination. Through a shared learning that sisterhood is both beautiful and powerful, women can join men as partners in recognizing that servanthood is beautiful and powerful for those who accept from Christ both its risk and its cost!

Humanization and diakonia. Diakonia is an indication of what it means to become more truly human by freely giving one's life for others. Part of the process of becoming more fully human is striving to participate in shaping the world in which a person lives, and being accepted as a *subject* and not as a thing or object of someone else's manipulation.[31] Once women discover a deeper understanding of sisterhood, they may also come to a deeper understanding of servanthood as an expression of the humanizing and liberating process. When women speak of liberation they are not trying to reverse the situation of oppression and to become new oppressors. They are simply asking the right and privilege of shaping their own life-styles in the modern world.[32]

The process of humanization which includes women and men is described in the Bible by the word *diakonia*; *diakonia* in the sense of taking responsibility before God on behalf of ourselves and our sisters and brothers in the work of Christ. It is the calling of God to partnership with others in God's liberating and humanizing work of justice, freedom, and peace. Thus Jesus' call to ministry, or *diakonia*, is described in Luke 4:18–19 as one of bringing Good News to the poor; release to the captives, setting at liberty those that are oppressed. . . . We serve because God has served us. We are set free by God to serve others and to become more fully ourselves, more fully human.

Partners in Christ's Church

It is not easy for women or men to find a way to be true partners in the church, especially because the church has for such a long time been considered *man's* church.[33] Yet we know that in the Holy Spirit it has been possible in other ages and is possible in our own. Even as Prisca and Aquila of Rome labored as co-partners with Paul in God's mission, we can also become co-partners in that mission to the world of today (Rom. 16:3).

When I graduated from Harvard Divinity School in 1958 and went to serve as a pastor in the East Harlem Protestant Parish in New York City, I invited one of my Harvard professors, Paul Lehmann, to preach my ordination sermon. When he got up to preach he announced his text as 1 Corinthians 14:34, "the women should keep silence in the churches." For a long half-hour I waited to see if indeed my ordination could go forward! Finally, having amassed as much evidence as possible against my ordination, he concluded that we could risk disobeying the Bible and proceed with my ordination because we must be open to the Holy Spirit and respond where the gifts of the Spirit are found.

Isn't this what women and ministry are all about? As Hewitt and Hiatt say, also following words of Paul, "Don't quench the Spirit" (1 Thess. 5:19).[34] Both women and men are called by Christ. Both women and men receive gifts of the Spirit (*charismata*). Now is the time to use these gifts on behalf of God's purpose of human liberation. "For freedom Christ has set us free" (Gal. 5:1).

Regardless of the structures of society or the church which stand in our way, our calling in Christ is to use the gifts God has given us as co-partners in Christ's work, so that God's will is done on earth as it is in heaven (Matt. 6:10).

NOTES

1. The material in this chapter is developed further in a book by Letty M. Russell on the subject of "Human Liberation in a Feminist Perspective" to be published by Westminster Press in 1974.
2. Hans Küng, *The Church,* trans. Ray and Rosaleen Ockenden (New York: Sheed & Ward, 1967); Hans Küng, *Why Priests?,* trans. Robert C. Collins (Garden City, New York: Doubleday, 1972); Raymond E. Brown, *Priest and Bishop: Biblical Reflections* (New York: Paulist Press, 1970); H. Richard Niebuhr, Daniel Day Williams and James Gustafson, *The Advancement of Theological Education* (New York: Harper & Row, 1957); Charles R. Fielding, *Education for Ministry* (Dayton: American Association of Theological Schools, 1966); "Theological Curriculum for the 1970's," *Theological Education* (Spring, 1968), IV:3, pp. 668-734; Steven G. Mackie, *Patterns of Ministry* (London: Collins, 1969).

3. Letty M. Russell, "Tradition as Mission: Study of a New Current in Theology and Its Implication for Theological Education" (unpublished doctoral dissertation, Union Theological Seminary, 1969), p. 263.
4. Anthony T. Hanson, *The Pioneer Ministry* (London: SCM Press, 1969), pp. 85-87; Küng, *The Church,* p. 383; Walter Abbott and Joseph Pallagher, eds., *The Documents of Vatican II* (New York: Guild Press, 1966), p. 27.
5. H. Richard Niebuhr, Daniel Day Williams, eds., *The Ministry in Historical Perspective* (New York: Harper & Row, 1956), pp. 19-21; Küng, *The Church,* pp. 402, 404-405.
6. Lewis S. Mudge, ed., *Model for Ministry: A Report for Study Issued by the General Assembly Special Committee on the Theology of the Call* (Philadelphia: Office of the General Assembly, United Presbyterian Church, USA, 1970).
7. *Work Book for the Assembly Committees,* Uppsala, 1968 (Geneva: World Council of Churches, 1968) "Patterns of Ministry," p. 128; T. W. Manson, T*he Church's Ministry* (London: Hodder & Stoughton, 1948), p. 81; Colin Williams, *The Church,* Vol. IV of *New Directions in Theology Today* (Philadelphia: The Westminster Press, 1968), p. 127; Joseph Fichter, "The Myth of the Hyphenated Clergy," *The Critic,* XXVIII:3 (December, 1968-January, 1969) pp., 16-24.
8. Emily Hewitt and Susan Hiatt, *Women Priests: Yes or No?* (New York: The Seabury Press, 1973). See also Resolution 12 (Consilium Congress, 12/17/9/70, Brussels): "The Discrimination which is practiced with regard to women in the Church as also often still in society must be denounced. It is time to consider the place of women in the ministries" (143 in favor; 21 against; 13 abstentions). Quoted from *Women in Ministry,* edited by S. Ethne Kennedy (Chicago: National Assembly of Women Religious, 1972), p. 34, footnote 22.
9. Kennedy, *Women in Ministry,* p. 34.
10. Two ecumenical groups of women are in the process of formation which will be designed to provide united strategies in this area of concern: The Women's Ecumenical Coordinating Group sponsored jointly by the Education for Development Office, of the NCC, by the Joint Strategy and Action Committee (JASAC), and by Church Women United; The Center for Development for Creative Ministries for Women being proposed by Church Employed Women of the United Presbyterian Church USA, Linda Brebner and Annette Wall, co-chairwomen.

11. Russell, p. 265.
12. Mary Daly, "The Courage to See: Religious Implications of the New Sisterhood," *The Christian Century* (September 22, 1971), pp. 1108-1111.
13. J.A.T. Robinson, *The New Reformation?* (Philadelphia: The Westminster Press, 1965), pp. 55-57.
14. Mudge, *Model for Ministry*.
15. Robinson, pp. 55-57.
16. Third World people is used here to refer to people living outside of the U.S.A. and Western Europe (the First World) and of the Communist bloc countries in Eastern Europe (the Second World), and also to their descendants living in racial oppression in the U.S.A. along with the Native Americans. The term is presently used by groups in the U.S.A. as a way of emphasizing that non-white groups are the *majority* of the world's population although they are a minority among those who hold political, social, and economic power. Full representation in the structures of the established white denominations in the U.S.A. by Third World people would call for radical changes in structures and requirements for ministry.
17. Niebuhr, pp. 1-3; Küng, *The Church,* p. 179.
18. Daniel Jenkins, *The Protestant Ministry* (Garden City, N.Y.: Doubleday, 1958), p. 38.
19. Niebuhr, p. 139; Robert C. Johnson, ed., *The Church and Its Changing Ministry* (Philadelphia: United Presbyterian Church USA, 1968), pp. 55, 60, 62.
20. Russell, pp. 254–268.
21. Hewitt and Hiatt, p. 52.
22. "Biblical Anthropology and the Participation of Women in the Ministry of the Church" (Geneva: World Council of Churches, 1964), p. 30.
23. All Biblical quotations are from the Revised Standard Version (New York: Thomas Nelson and Sons. 1952).
24. Oscar Cullmann, "Jesus the Suffering Servant of God," in *The Christology of the New Testament,* trans. Shirley C. Guthrie and Charles A. McHall (Philadelphia: The Westminster Press, 1959), pp. 51-82.
25. Letty M. Russell, "Women's Liberation in a Biblical Perspective," *Concern* (May-June, 1971), 13:5, p. 17.
26. Ferdinand Klostermann, *Das Christliche Apostolat* (Innsbruck, 1962), pp. 108 ff.
27. Küng, *The Church,* p. 437. John Calvin, *Institutes of the Christian*

Religion, 7th ed., trans. John Allen (Philadelphia: Board of Christian Education), IV:IV:9.

28. Paulo Freire, *Pedagogy of the Oppressed,* trans. Myra Bergman Ramos (New York: Herder and Herder, 1970), pp. 19, 95, 101.
29. Paulo Freire, *Education for Critical Consciousness* (New York: Seabury Press, 1973), p. 44.
30. Karl Barth, *Church Dogmatics: A Selection,* trans. G. W. Bromiley (New York: Harper & Row, 1961), p. 228.
31. Freire, *Pedagogy of the Oppressed,* pp. 42, 91.
32. Rosemary Radford Ruether, *Liberation Theology* (New York: Paulist Press, 1972), p. 13.
33. Arlene Swidler, *Woman in Man's Church* (New York: Paulist Press, 1972).
34. Hewitt and Hiatt, p. 101.

BLACK WOMEN AND THE CHURCHES:
Triple Jeopardy

Theressa Hoover

To be a woman, black, and active in religious institutions in the American scene is to labor under triple jeopardy.

It is a well-accepted fact that women in America, though in the majority statistically, are generally in inferior positions. Economically they are at the bottom of the ladder in terms of those receiving high-paying salaries. Politically, although they have the possibility of more voters being women, they have not yet experienced the full potential of that vote. Women constitute a very small number of the persons in political office at all levels of the nation's life. Religiously, though they comprise more than 50 per cent of the churches' membership, they are by no means at the higher levels of decision-making in the churches.

It has long been an established fact in American life that color is a deterrent to high achievement; not because there is inherent inferiority but because societal conditions predetermine lower achievement. Thus, while every woman in America faces economic and political discrimination, a woman who is black has an added barrier.

Religion in American society is often espoused, even in high places, but it is not yet the warp and woof of our actions. The woman who is vitally involved with religious institutions in our society must take on responsibilities often not accepted by others.

To confront the inequities of women and the inequities of blacks, and to have the responsibilities of a dedication to the church, is triple jeopardy for a black woman. There is very little written which brings together these three elements. There is little or no mention of black women in accounts of any black church or black theology and in the *Ebony* special issue on "The Negro Woman" (August 1960) she is treated in every way except in the area of religion. *The Making of Black Revolutionaries* by James Forman and *Black Women in White America* by Gerda Lerner, both published in 1972, are the only books available which give a bit more dimension to the strength and courage of black Christian women now and in the past. Any thinking person cannot help wondering why so little has been written, since women are by far the largest supporting groups in our religious institutions, and, in the black church, are the very backbone.

We know too well the debates going on in the American religious institutions about women—their role, their access to all privileges and responsibilities in the priestly hierarchy, their representation in decision-making places, and their total condition in these institutions. Apparently no one has seen the plight of American black women in the religious institutions of our society. One might conclude that where something is written about women in general in these institutions black women are included. This may be true, but it is not the total picture. Even in the predominantly all-white denominations, the black woman commonly finds herself in black local congregations. Judged by what is written in the historic black denominations the black woman is invisible.

Black Women: The Backbone of the Black Churches

Some people hallow the black church, citing evidence of the hope such churches could give their communities if they had the financial support of a larger group. Others detract from the past and belittle the future potential of the black church in the black community, claiming these churches have become little more than middle-class social clubs, out of contact with the real hurts of people in their communities. The detractors use caricatures of a black preacher riding around town in his Cadillac purchased by gifts from welfare checks or chicken dinners sold by black women of his congregation. There is probably truth in both the compliment and the caricature: the black church which properly assesses the potential of its community, and applies its resources to that potential, can be the better servant of the community. The preacher in the black church *is* more directive, authoritarian, and singular in his administration. The degree to which he uses his position selfishly marks the amount of personal privilege and reward he enjoys at the expense of a "not so well endowed" membership—the majority of which are women.

This situation has sociological and psychological explanations. In the post-slavery period, the black church was the only place in the community where economic well-being was dependent on direct black giving. In many situations the preacher had to play the roles of social worker and political and religious adviser. To perform properly he had to have enough ability to get on with the powers at city hall or in the county courthouse. In town after town—even in the Deep South—he was the only black man not referred to as "George" or "boy." He was called "Rev." or "Preacher." Such courtesy did not necessarily concede he was a man, but that he was a little more than "boy."

Many of today's major black churches have their roots in protest. Richard Allen walked out of the Methodist Episcopal Church in Philadelphia rather than accept segregation at the communion table, and the African Methodist Episcopal Church is a monument to that protest. Countless hundreds of local Methodist and Baptist congregations across the country have kept alive that protest. They were the churches that provided succor to the slave family, that also helped them accommodate to earthly travail with the promise of a better life in the hereafter. Today many criticize this role of the past. Given a similar oppressive situation, however, would we have done otherwise? During the same period some churches were the places where insurrectionists gathered to plan strategies and attacks.

In the 1960s during the civil rights struggle there were black ministers in leadership in difficult places and situations. With them were women and men who had come under the teaching of the gospel in the churches and had believed. Churches were the targets of the racists' bombs and guns. In some ways, they were targets more than any other institutions, since the schools—probably the only other places in the community which could accommodate the crowds—were the property of the Establishment. The black church was of the black community, owned by it and sustained by it, and thus it became the target of the racists. Joseph R. Washington, Jr., illustrates the point well:

In the beginning was the black church, and the black church was with the black community, and the black church was the black community. The black church was in the beginning with the black people; all things were made through the black church, and without the black church was not anything that was made. In the black church was life, and the life was the light of the black people. The black church still shines in the darkness and the darkness has not overcome it.[1]

Lest it be thought that this is a valid description of the black church in black Southern communities only, the experience of Cicely Tyson, who grew up in New York City, should be noted:

We were in church Sunday morning to Saturday night. It was our whole life, our social life, our religious training, everything. My mother didn't believe in movies, so I didn't go to the movies. . . . But I enjoyed the church services. I sang in the choir and played the piano and the organ. Sometimes when my mother worked late at night, Nana would take my sister and my brother and me to the Baptist church. It was that kind of thing that saved us. Church became a shelter for us. A lot of kids growing up with us are not here today because of drugs or alcohol, or they died some violent death. They weren't necessarily bad kids.[2]

During the period 1948 to 1958 I traveled eleven months out of each year, all across the United States. I spent those years in and out of every major city, in countless small towns, and on the back roads in open country. Needless to say, hospitality for me in those days was always arranged for in the home of some black Methodist family. The only able-bodied, employed male I observed at home during the weekdays was the pastor. For some it was an escape into a natural or acquired laziness. For others it was an opportunity to read, study, and join with other clergymen in talking of their dilemmas, boasting of last Sunday's offerings, or strategizing about some community need.

During those ten years of travel I discovered that black women were truly the glue that held the churches together. The women worked, yet found time to be the Sunday school teachers, sing in the choir, and support the church's program in every way. The women found the time and energy to be active in the women's missionary societies and to serve as counselors or sponsors for the youth group. They were the domestics of the community and the teachers in the black schools. The latter were often either hometown girls or ones who had grown up in a town similar to the one in which they now worked and boarded with a respectable family. The church was their "home away from home," the social orbit in which they met the right people.

The minister's wife deserves special mention. She often worked outside the home, too, depending on the financial status of the church her husband served. In many cases she gave piano lessons—or did sewing for a little change if she was lucky. She was sometimes a teacher in the nearby country school. On occasion she, too, joined the long line of domestics leaving her end of town to spend part of the day at work in homes on the other side of town. She was still expected to prepare her family's meals, clean the parsonage, and do the allotted amount of church work.

In most of these communities the blacks were either Methodists or Baptists. The Methodists were a mixture. Some belonged to a primarily white denomination even though they found the local expression in black congregations. Others belonged to one of the three primarily black Methodist denominations—African Methodist Episcopal, African Methodist Episcopal Zion, or Christian Methodist Episcopal. All, however, were related to a connectional system, meaning that they had a presiding elder who was their link to other churches in the denomination and to a bishop who linked them to a still larger judicatory of the denomination. The Baptists tended to belong to a fellowship of Baptists, but each local church was autonomous. History has produced many varieties: there were progressive and independent; there were Antioch and Shiloh.

In both Baptist and Methodist churches the women were the backbone, the "glue." They were present at the midweek prayer services, the Monday-afternoon women's missionary meetings, and the Sunday morning, afternoon, and evening preaching services. Rarely has there been in the black church a great distinction between men and women holding office or sharing in decision-making in the local churches.

Missions as Focus for Contact and Cooperation

In the 1950s, women in the various Methodist groups began to discover one another. While there had been a sharing of programs and other resources in many local communities, there had been no real coming-together nationally. The women of the basically white Methodist Church had a joint committee with the women of the basically black Christian Methodist Episcopal (CME) Church. The relationship was still in the realm of a "missionary project" on the part of the white denomination, for it was they who provided the staff help, the printed resources, and the money to assure leadership training for the women of the CME Church. The two groups have since moved into an era of more equitable contribution to the joint experiment. Coming together later as co-units in the World Federation of Methodist Women, they extended the fellowship to include women of the African Methodist Episcopal and the African Methodist Episcopal Zion churches.

Each of the four Methodist women's groups has a history of mission work in this country and overseas. They have supported their own programs even as they have aided the mission outreach of the denomination in which they were a part. These women's missionary groups developed out of the desire of women to be involved with the hurts, needs, and potential of women everywhere. The regular mission channels of the denominations were controlled by the clergy to the point of the deliberate exclusion of women. To give expression to the needs felt by women the women's missionary society was organized as a parallel or auxiliary group. That felt need and that exclusion from main church channels still exist. Today these groups of women are strong numerically and financially.

The nationally organized churchwomen's groups active today are: the African Methodist Episcopal Church Women's Missionary Society, the African Methodist Episcopal Zion Church Women's Home and Missionary Society, the Christian Methodist Episcopal Church Women's Missionary Council, the Women's Auxiliary of the National Baptist Convention, and the United Methodist Women's Division.

There are varying degrees of autonomy in these organizations. Each is a recognized body of the denomination which makes possible the functioning of the group at all levels of the church's life. The groups range in size from two thousand to thirty thousand local units in the United States with a combined membership in the millions.

United Methodist Women, part of a Board of Global Ministries, retains the constitutional right to enlist women as members, to provide program and educational materials, and to secure and expend funds. It is the largest remaining mainline churchwomen's group with that degree of autonomy. It has some thirty thousand local units.

Black Women and the Black Manifesto

In the late 1960s the religious institutions in America toward which the Black Manifesto was directed were in disarray. The legally achieved integration of the early sixties had been found wanting in quality and in practice. For the liberal white integrationists, the apparent move toward separatism, signaled by the Black Power movement and culminating in the Manifesto of 1969, was mind-blowing to say the least. To some, separatism represented a threat or a cop-out.

Not long after the Black Manifesto was made public I was called by the executive director of Church Women United to a conference to discuss what impact this move would have on black women in that organization. My counsel to her then, later borne out, was that it would produce no "break-off" though it might well call forth some soul searching as to the seriousness with which women honor our differences and pool our resources and resourcefulness on behalf of all.

Nevertheless, to test my counsel, Church Women United called a small consultation of black churchwomen in September, 1969, at Wainwright House, Rye, New York, to consider their role and expectations in the aftermath of the Black Manifesto. The group concluded that churchwomen—black and white—must function under the limitations of religious thought and practice. This fact alone was sufficiently limiting; there was no purpose to be served by further splintering ourselves along the lines of race.

We talked about the role women can play in the total life of the church, about the areas the church has not yet given evidence of serving, about the gap between mainline black churchwomen and their younger black sisters. Most of us represented the former category. We were the ones who attended the colleges set up by the churches to educate the recently freed slaves and had gone on to become teachers in them or staff in their national headquarters. We had little experience with overt assignment of women to second-class posts in churches, largely because we were so vitally needed if churches were even to exist. We were the ones who had been taught and had accepted a role on behalf of "our people" even if it meant foregoing a personal life exemplified in husband and children. We were the ones who, if married at all, had married "beneath us"—meaning that we had married men with less education who did manual labor. (Note the influence of white society's value system.) This was not true for the young black woman of the late 1960s.

These are some of the remarks heard at that weekend consultation:

"The young black's mistake is in not making enough of their American experience. We will never be Africans. In slavery only the strong and those with a will to live survived—those with spiritual resiliency."

"Black people once thought education was the answer; they found it wasn't. Now they think economics is the answer; we'll find it won't be, either. We have to find something else—we have to deal with the attitude of people on the top in order to solve this. As churchwomen and as black women, how can we do this?"

"Women have always taken care of everyone's problems and have been left behind. Women must be free before they can begin to make decisions."

"To accomplish a specific goal, an organized minority can bring about change. It is not necessary to have great numbers."

"Women must be accepted as persons. The black man wants to assert today his so-called masculinity, but it is really *personhood*—for both sexes."

"So far as young women versus men are concerned, let the men have their power and status; we organize the women's caucus; when the men are ready for our help, they will have to bargain for it."

Ethnic Caucuses in White Churches

Ethnic caucuses in white denominations sprang up in the aftermath of the civil rights struggle. The soil had been prepared for their advent. It took an act of national significance to release the simmering disenchantment of minority groups with their place in white denominations. What is interesting is the role and status of women within the ethnic caucuses.

Not unlike the role of women in the civil rights struggle of the sixties women in the caucuses have been assigned (and have accepted) a supportive role. Most of the decision-makers have been men, primarily clergymen. It might help to look closely at the "life and growth of caucuses" in a major mainline denomination whose membership is a replica of the nation at large. Let's take the United Methodist Church (which has 54 per cent women members) as a case study.

1. At the 1966 Special Session of General Conference of the Methodist Church, with the Evangelical United Brethren Church Conference in session across the hall, there was only one visible caucus, Methodists for Church Renewal. This caucus cut across race and sex lines, though the dominant group consisted of white male clergy.

2. At the regular Methodist General Conference in 1968 (with the Evangelical United Brethren Church holding a simultaneous Special Session), a second caucus was present, Black Methodists for Church Renewal (BMCR). At this session the union of the two denominations was consummated and, with it, the official end of the Methodist all-Negro Central Jurisdiction. In February, 1968, just two months prior to the General Conference, over two hundred black Methodists had gathered in Cincinnati, Ohio. They came from the Far West and East, where structural segregation included only the local church; from the Middle West (Illinois to Colorado, Missouri to Kentucky), where conferences had already been merged with their white counterparts; and from the Southwest and Southeast, where no noticeable change was in the offing. While it was church renewal that brought them together, it was their blackness which made the gathering imperative.

Black clergymen were by far the majority of those attending, but a real effort was made to get lay men and women. Both were there. Strategically, many of them would be voting delegates in the upcoming General Conference. The national board of directors elected before the conference closed totaled forty-four, with nine women, a number not commensurate with black women's presence or support in black churches—but an action taken without recourse to pressure by women.

One directive to the board of directors says something about the group's awareness of the black woman. They were directed to "employ an assistant director which shall be a woman, *if* the executive director is a man." There was not the assumption, which is so often true, that the director would be a man. Instead, it was an assurance that the leadership of the staff would reflect the talents of both male and female.

Black women and men, lay and clerical, were visible at the luncheons, after-hours caucuses, and the on-floor debate at the General Conference. As a result, our denomination created and funded a Commission on Religion and Race. When the Commission was organized and staffed, however, there were no guarantees for the participation of women, and the Commission cannot be applauded for their involvement. In fact, it is fair to say that women have been generally disregarded in its life and work. So the struggle must go on.

3. At the 1970 Special General Conference, still another caucus, youthful United Methodists, secured the right to self-determination.

4. At the 1972 General Conference the youth caucus was the only caucus that included women in the warp and woof of its proceedings and decision-making. Black Methodists for Church Renewal, barely visible and still masculine and clerical, saw the rise of a women's caucus in its own ranks before it got the message that "coalition around common interests" was not only desirable but imperative.

The newest caucus—the women's caucus—was a great new fact. Black women were among its members and took active roles. Representatives of the BMCR women's caucus were a bridge so that BMCR, the women's caucus, and the Youth-Young Adult Caucus formed a working coalition to achieve common goals. As a result a Commission on the Status and Role of Women was created and funded, though not to the desired degree. The Commission has organized with a black woman as its chairperson. The effort brought together still another interesting phenomenon—the joint effort of young, unorganized women with the older, organized women's group in the denomination.

Judith Hole and Ellen Levine in their book *Rebirth of Feminism* say:

Feminist activities within the Christian community most often fall into three categories: (1) challenging the theological view of women; (2) challenging the religious laws and/or customs which bar women from ordination; (3) demanding that the professional status and salaries of women in the church be upgraded.[3]

These categories may apply to the total feminist movement in the churches, but do not yet reflect the view of many black women. First, the economic necessity of the black woman's efforts on behalf of her church has not pressured her to the point of accepting the prevailing theological view of women. When she gets a little release from other church pressures, she will look beyond her local church and realize that such theological views and practices are operative both in her exclusion from doctrinal decision-making and in her absence from national representation.

Second, in the predominantly black churches women are not excluded from ordination by law, though they may be in practice. Third, most of the black denominations are not financially capable of maintaining even a minimal professional staff (outside the clerical hierarchy). Where there is staff, women already know the necessity of insisting on comparable salaries.

Most of the women in such staff positions—not unlike those in their more wealthy sister churches—tend to be related to the women's missionary groups and/or the church's educational agencies. Most of the national presidents receive a nominal cash stipend for the administrative work they do in the absence of a staff. The other most likely staff position is as the editor of the women's paper or the women's column in the denominational paper.

In 1967 the national Woman's Division (the Methodist Church) held a consultation of Negro women. The focus was on Negro women in merged situations. From the findings I have excerpted the following expectations the women brought: "What can be done in situations where there has been desegregation but no integration? How can we somehow deflate the superiority complex in the white woman and help to eliminate the inferiority complex in the nonwhite? What can we do to recognize good judgment, and respect it, in the noneducated woman?"

In 1968 a survey was made of Methodist leadership in merged structures.[4] Interpretive comments based on the response, elicited through a questionnaire distributed across the organization, speak to the dilemma of black leadership in white churches.

This inquiry (or survey) was planned as a broad-based, though focused, review of progress made toward integrating hitherto racially separated structures. It was not designed as a statistical inquiry. Generalizations made by the research team were:

1. It was not found that enlightenment regarding other ethnic groups is a product of geographical location.

2. It was not demonstrated that size of locality determines the nature and extent of "progress" toward successful integration.

3. It was not manifest that membership in any particular ethnic group controls or determines readiness for either "merger" or "integration."

"Merger" was an area of misconception. A number of replies indicate that this was commonly thought of as the process through which the racial or ethnic minorities were to give up their identities.

"Integrated merger" was a concept employed by a few who saw the previously separated groups as coming together in one "mix," to which each would contribute and for which each would yield some of its former prerogatives, comforts, and complacencies.

At this writing only one of the jurisdictional women's groups out of the five regional jurisdictions has a black president; two have black vice-presidents.

In February 1972, a National Black Women's Conference was called by Mrs. Elizabeth M. Scott, president of Black Women's Association. It met in Pittsburgh. In its section on "Role of Black Woman in the Community," there are conclusions and suggestions for actions that at least make some acknowledgement of the black woman in her church. One reads: "The church must be a meeting place for different people of the community, a place to listen to the problems of the community, a place for planning better opportunities for the people of the community." In its action section there are two references to black women as church women. "We, the black churchwomen, must move our churches to serve as a meeting place to provide the opportunity for volunteers, e.g., tutoring, detection of learning deficiencies, supervision, planning skills, leadership." And the following: "Black women must get on policy making boards (both secular and sacred) in the community and serve in executive positions. . . ."

Black Women—Strengthened by Faith

The black churchwoman must come to the point of challenging

both her sisters in other denominations and the clerical-male hierarchy in her own. In many ways she has been the most oppressed and the least vocal. She has given the most and, in my judgment, gotten the least. She has shown tremendous faithfulness to the spirit of her church. Her foresight, ingenuity, and "stick-to-itiveness" have kept many black churches open, many black preachers fed, many parsonages livable.

She has borne her children in less than desirable conditions, managed her household often in the absence of a husband. She has gathered unto herself the children of the community, she has washed them, combed their hair, fed them and told them Bible stories—in short, she has been their missionary, their substitute mother, their teacher. Many leaders of the present-day black church owe their commitment to the early influence of just such a black woman.

You may have heard of the Church of the Black Madonna in Detroit, Michigan. While I do not know how it came to be so named, I would guess that it is not to be confused with the usual "pedestal placing" of woman—above the fray protected, adorned, and excluded! I choose to see it as homage to black women—their numbers, their strength, their faith, their sustaining and prophetic role in the black church.

In James Forman's book, referred to earlier, there is a chapter on "Strong Black Women." Forman speaks to the heart that women bring to the black church, indeed to the entire religious community, in references to women in the Albany, Georgia, protest of the 1960s.

> The strength of the women overwhelmed me. Here they were in jail, but their spirits seemed to rise each minute. They were yelling at the jailer, cursing, singing, ready to fight if someone came to their cell to mistreat them. Images of other strong black women resisting slavery and servitude flooded my mind. I thought of Georgia Mae Turner and Lucretia Collins and the young girls in the cell block next to me now as the modern-day Harriet Tubmans, Sojourner Truths, and all those proud black women who did not allow slavery to break their spirits. . . . As I thought about the women protesting their arrest, I knew that the black liberation movement would escalate, for too many young people were involved. Most of the women in the cells were very young, one of them only fourteen.[5]

With such a heritage of strength and faith, black women in the churches today must continue strong in character and in faith. They must reach other sisters and brothers with a sense of the commonality of their struggles on behalf of black people, and ultimately all humanity. They must continue to work within the "walls" of the church, challenging theological pacesetters and church bureaucrats; they also must continue to push outward the church "walls" so it may truly serve the black community. They must be ever aware of their infinite worth, their godliness in the midst of creatureliness, and their having been freed from the triple barriers of *sex, race,* and *church* into a community of believers.

NOTES

1. Joseph R. Washington, Jr., "How Black Is Black Religion?" in *Quest for a Black Theology,* eds. James J. Gardiner, S.A., and J. Deotis Roberts, Sr. (Philadelphia: Pilgrim Press, 1970), p. 28.
2. Cicely Tyson, *The New York Times,* October 1, 1972.
3. Judith Hole and Ellen Levine, *Rebirth of Feminism* (New York: Quadrangle Books, 1971), p. 377.
4. A survey within Women's Societies of Christian Service and Wesleyan Service Guilds (the Methodist Church) by Research and Action, Inc., New York City, 1968.
5. James Forman, *The Making of Black Revolutionaries* (New York: Macmillan Co., 1972), p. 200.

RELIGIOUS SOCIALIZATION OF WOMEN WITHIN U.S. SUBCULTURES

Gwen Kennedy Neville

In approaching the formidable topic of religious socialization, I will concentrate on three central issues in the process by which women are enculturated into set roles in our society. One is *learning*—the subtle process of acquiring all the necessary behaviors to act out successfully the role of "woman" within a particular community's way of life.

The second issue is *culture*. I have included the phrase "within U.S. subcultures" in the title of this essay because I want to disavow any belief in the abstract construct of an "American culture" overall, or even of a WASP culture. "White Anglo-Saxon Protestant" is simply a label for a category of people, lumped together because they would share these four traits if they were printed out on someone's computer. (Jewish or Catholic with any three variables added would also print out numbers and distributions and give us a stack of census cards.) Cultural and social categories are interesting, but it is not within general labels that people learn to be male or female. They learn these meanings and behaviors within real human groups. *Cultural groups* are made up of interacting webs of real people involved in personal kin and religious relationships extending over a transgenerational time period and over a particular geographical space. I have spoken of these groups within American society as subcultures because they exist as *internal systems* within the larger systems of the metropolis and of the national body politic. They are sometimes invisible but emerge to express commonality at special times. As socializing agents cultural groups are formidable in their effectiveness.

The third item on the agenda is *liberation*. It has been so much bandied about that probably all of us wonder if anything new remains to be said. We wonder, if we understand the tenacity of culture, whether liberation is possible. If it is, I hope to look at some alternative cultural arrangements that may enable and accompany liberated life-styles.

Framing the Question

In 1966, somewhere on the road to liberation, I asked a very liberated friend of mine how she had become so free. This particular friend had completed her B.D. at a fine theological seminary, served as an associate pastor in California, had taken part in the early student movement, and had married a bright young classmate who also was a pastor. She was intelligent, charming, and had a good job doing interesting things. So, interested in ascertaining how she had broken out of her very traditional cultural past in Tennessee, I asked, "How did you get so free?"

She replied, after some thought, "I think I just read the Bible and believed it."

After six years, I crossed paths again with the same woman. She was now a housewife and mother, working in volunteer groups while her husband taught on the faculty of a southern state university. Both had been honor students at seminary. *He* went back for a Ph.D., while she had two babies. *He* interviewed nationally and found a good job as an assistant professor, while she moved with him. *He* writes lectures, books, articles, thinks about important things, while she donates her time at the church and at the McGovern headquarters and plans to get back to school "someday when the children are a little older." What had happened to the freedom? to believing the Bible? It looked as if cultural programming had been effective. Tennessee had won, in the last analysis.

I had seen it happen to one after another of my friends and to myself in intermittent doses. We had each one "believed it"—the Bible, the public-school party line about all individuals being equal, the national political speeches about giving the same opportunities to all. At the conscious, rational level we were all raised to believe that we should seek an education and that we could be anything we wanted to be. Many girls I knew had gone to college and on to graduate school. But somewhere along the way, by the time of the tenth high-school reunion, all the boys had miraculously turned into orthodontists and veterinarians, and petroleum engineers, and most of the girls had simply turned into mommies. Something had happened that I couldn't explain. Something invisible was going on that had sabotaged everyone's good intentions. The search for an explanation has continued to occupy me as I miraculously, after already becoming a mommie, have turned into an anthropologist.

Learning

With the best of intentions, thousands of girls graduate from college every year and start out merrily on jobs. Thousands of others finish graduate school, become physicians and lawyers. Their teachers have praised them and encouraged them to their best ability and they have believed of themselves that they are "different" and will be able to suceed at having a career, possibly combining it with marriage and a family. Many succeed but under great disadvantages and with a great deal more guilt and conflict than they had ever dreamed would be necessary.

Others succumb to the demands of culture—embodied in their mothers and aunts and husbands and their inner consciences. It is so much easier to do it "their way." For even the most liberated of active professional women, after all, has a mother. And the mother, in addition to being very proud of her daughter's success, will be very worried about her own grandchildren's welfare. She will most certainly appoint herself as personal reminder to the daughter that she is lucky to have such a good husband who "lets her continue working." Or, even more common is the mother who continually warns the daughter that if she doesn't watch out she will "lose her husband to another woman who will treat him with more attention and indulgence and not boss him around so much."

Every woman has, in addition to her mother, aunts and grandmothers in the wings somewhere, a mother-in-law if she is married, and then of course her husband's aunts and grandmothers. Then there are all the assorted fathers, step-fathers, uncles, and brothers who have assigned themselves the task of spoiling the little girl and keeping the big girl in line. Even in the comic strip Dennis the Menace, Gina is seen explaining to Joey that he has to be a proper brother to his new baby sister and "see that she marries the right guy." The process of invisible induction into culturally-approved ways begins in the bassinet.

Through the handling and treatment of little girls and little boys, the way they are dressed and the toys they are given, we know that culture is transmitted in invisible ways. E. T. Hall[1] calls this "the silent language"—the language of actions and relationships that in early years speaks loud instructions to girls and boys of how they must act out their social roles.

In looking closely at this learning process, one can see several principles clearly at work in shaping sex roles and transmitting cultural expectations:

1. The first principle has to do with levels of learning. Women in our society are socialized on two levels—the verbal, rational public level (what teachers and parents and churches *say*) and the invisible, behavioral, private level (what teachers and parents and churches *do*). At the conscious level, my friend's clergyman probably stood up for human liberation. Her mother encouraged her to make good grades in school. Meanwhile, at home other signals were communicated to her so efficiently that at the proper moment, when triggered by certain cues, she voluntarily gave up her own career for her husband's and began the cycle of being a mother. Psychological studies have demonstrated the persistency of these learning experiences. From the point of view of the student of culture, the reason for this persistency of early learning is that it takes place within a religious-kin unit.

It is in this group that the individual finds his or her identity and receives the set of *cultural instructions* that enable a child to become an adult among that people. In less complex societies, of course, the kin-religious network was coterminous with geographic community. In an urbanized world, the community has gone underground. Now the religious-kin community establishes itself only periodically and is otherwise scattered into nuclear dwelling units.

2. Growing out of this understanding, a second principle could be stated as follows: Women learn their expected roles through interaction in a specific subcultural community. Each subcultural group will have its own styles of participation for men and women. Each sex will have assigned tasks and activities that are required and others that are taboo. For instance, in a Protestant worship

service in the American Northeast the family group will be seated together in the same pew. In the same city at the orthodox synagogue, mothers and daughters will sit behind a screen so that the men and boys will not see them and be distracted from the serious business of prayers. Girls growing up in each of these traditions may attend public schools and be taught the same amalgamated American virtues. But their social realities are very different from one another and from those purveyed in the school textbook.

The ethnicity of Jewish, Italian, Irish, American Indian, and Mexican-American peoples has been widely recognized. Communities of each of these groups are dispersed over the regions of the country and distributed up and down the social strata. The same internal segmentation has not been widely described, however, for the subcultures within white Protestantism. My own research has been directed recently to the establishment of criteria for defining ethnic subgroups within the white Protestant population—a phenomenon I call Anglo-Saxon Ethnicity. I have described one such group in an ethnography of a Southern Presbyterian summer community composed of individuals of Scottish descent. I am convinced there are a multiplicity of other such communities existing at high holy seasons within Christianity.

The existence of such gathered kin-religious networks is evident at Thanksgiving, when families feel obligated to get together, at Christmas, birthdays, or at school holidays and in the summer. The continent is a collage of overlapping webs of this type, varying by region, by class, and by ethnic background.

This gathering and dispersal of human groups is one of the identifying marks of a human community's viability over time. Another identifying mark is the presence of at least three generations, two sexes, and all the known types of actors to put on the play of that people's way of life.[2] Culture is transmitted to the child by all these people as they act out toward him or her their roles of "aunt," "uncle," "friend of the family," "parish minister," and so on, just doing what uncles and aunts do and expecting the child to do what nephews and nieces do. Within these activities a highly important transmission of culture is taking place.

3. A third principle of learning involves the transmission of culture within these ceremonies and rituals. Among the Cheyennes of the Great Plains, and a number of other peoples of the Americas,

families lived, as many Americans do, scattered about in the nuclear family units. During most of the year they were engaged in hunting and gathering activities. Then, at one specific prearranged time, all the separate bands would gather together for the celebration of the Sun Dance. Placing of the camps was symbolic of the social hierarchy, with certain places assigned to chiefs and set places for the various bands of the tribe. The enactment of the Sun Dance restated Cheyenne values about the natural world and their place in it. The dancing of the ritual and the food-sharing and visiting renewed patterns of cooperation for the following year, and young marriageable adults used the opportunity to find suitable marriage partners from suitable cooperating bands.

This type of gathering is called a rite of intensification,[3] because it serves to intensify the commitment of the participants to the values of the culture and to rehabituate them to acceptable social roles. The dual function of a rite of intensification is to achieve new commitment and to rehabituate participants. In order to do this, set forms will tend to repeat traditional patterns over and over again. For example, Thanksgiving dinner tends to be much more traditional in many families than any ordinary family meal. It includes set patterns of stereotyped behaviors: e.g., the dressing has to be made before the turkey is carved and it is *Mother* who makes the dressing and *Father* who carves the turkey. Passover is another good example of this type of tradition maintenance. The woman who keeps a kosher house may spend weeks cleaning, sorting, and putting away foods to satisfy dietary laws. Then she will spend days carrying out the observances. Daughters must help in this project and are informally given training through the interaction of all the rules and laws of the household.

Victor Turner,[4] drawing on his work in an East African society, points out that during rituals and ceremonial enactments the emotions are heightened and learning is intensified or speeded up. Turner attributes this condition to the fact that within religious ritual occasions, persons are drawn out of the highly ordered structures of the political and economic hierarchy and thrown together into a *communitas*. The reason that this particular principle takes on such significance is that in American subcultures, as in East Africa, the seasonal ritual and ceremonial gatherings are one of the principal vehicles for cultural persistency. At these times all the central, core values of each cultural group are acted out in time and space—all the values and beliefs and marriage patterns and holy observances that are necessary in order for that culture to survive as an entity. Ceremonials are a preservative of culture—and human beings cannot exist without a culture-community matrix. Inside the stereotyped events that go into preparing for Thanksgiving or Passover, a child learns what it means to be a woman or a man in that culture.

In a sort of mini-ritual, the same values and beliefs about women, men, and the world are acted out over again every week on Sunday morning at 11:00 A.M. or in Sabbath services on Friday night. Sitting behind the screen at the synagogue is a spatial enactment of the belief that women are inferior to men and that their presence too near the altar will pollute the holy paraphernalia. In Catholic masses the same spatial separation in which women are not allowed to come onto the altar or to administer the sacraments communicates to the child similar messages. In Protestant churches this space barrier has only recently been broken down regarding the sacraments and performance of sacred functions in worship, and as recently as ten years ago the general absence of women on church boards taught the little girl effectively that the business of the church was men's business. Their mommies' business was to organize church circles and family-night suppers in a separate, special, female arena of activity.

The fact that these messages have been well learned is exemplified by the number of women today in their twenties and thirties who want very much in their heads to be liberated and to break the mold. They want to try equal living within the church or the university but they suffer from frustration, conflict, and ulcers at the whole situation. No matter how much we desire interaction as equals, we fall into traps of saying we will make the coffee or take the minutes of the meeting. Our beliefs about reality have been programmed into us and stamped with supernatural approval.

In addition to learning through the space use and division of labor in these high ceremonial gatherings, the little girl is learning from the language used by the religious community. This is a language in which all references to the deity are couched in male pronouns and in which the hymns all refer blatantly to Christian soldiers or to men of God, verbally codifying the little girl's reality into a cognitive set which classifies her *out* of any meaningful participation. She is also exposed to word and picture language in Sunday-school curricula in which boys are active and assertive in doing interesting things and girls sit by and watch out of windows.[5] She is taught by a female teacher, who is a mommy, and she is preached to in the sanctuary by a male person who talks about "all Mankind" and the relation of God to Man. In Hebrew school, in much of Catholic education, and in many conservative Protestant groups, she is taught in a group of all girls after about the fourth grade, a group which learns that they will someday marry the boys in the other group and live happily ever after.

Culture

It is obvious that these aspects of learning are all tied up with aspects of culture. Learning can be legitimately defined, in one sense, simply as "cultural transmission."

What is transmitted, after all?

The answer is that society transmits a way of organizing reality into meaningful categories and assigning labels to things. The world view of a culture is expressed in its social arrangements and has its roots in the natural environmental niche to which the culture is adapted.

Now, since in the United States we are dealing with cultures that have been ripped out of their European environments and reinstated in new locations, the process of tracing becomes important. Anderson[6] and others have pointed out that European cultures have been translated into various denominations in our continent. Each defines the roles women should play in that specific cultural universe.

We can identify at least three European culture areas that have been transplanted into our denominational structures. One is the Mediterranean, brought to us in Italian and Spanish Catholicism. In this world view a highly ordered and hierarchical universe is acted out in a church hierarchy of all-male prelates. This is the original home of the "cult of the Virgin," a long tradition predating the Christian era of young girls who see holy visions. The protection of women is expressed in reverence for the position of holiness in motherhood, and the honor of the family and lineage is upheld by all.

The movie *Light in the Piazza* pointed this up in terms of the simple and nonparticipatory role of women in an Italian Catholic household. An American mother was faced with a decision, according to *TV Guide,* "of whether to allow her daughter, who was a beautiful twenty-six-year-old brain-injured daughter with the mind of a ten-year-old child, to marry an Italian boy of a fine family, or whether to put the child into a 'special school.'" The ironic thing about the story was that the mother never revealed to the boy or his parents that her daughter was not perfectly normal. They were charmed with her childlike qualities, delighted that he should find such a good, fine, gentle, and sweet girl for a wife. What the plot seemed to convey is that any intelligent and happy ten-year-old could fulfill the woman's role in a subculture holding a Mediterranean world view. Even the priest reported that she was "doing well in her instructions."

Southern England fell heir to this idealized version of woman along with the feudal adaptation of a plantation economy and the English vision of Christianity. The romantic images of women were accompanied by fortresses to keep arrows out and women in. This feudal-plantation system was transplanted to Virginia and South Carolina, and the "Southern lady" image has become part of a romantic American stereotype. The perpetuation of this image makes it difficult for women in the South even today to break loose and gain independence and professional equality. A shortage of professional women as job candidates characterizes a region so long tied up in the notion of "Southern womanhood."

The second form of religion and world view to be noted is that found in the people of the Middle European Plains. One well-known representative is the Anglo-Saxon village of Germany taken to the East Anglia region of England and onward into New England. The world view in this culture centers on the cooperative farming patterns needed to grow and harvest grain, and all adults participate equally in work activities. In this culture—brought to us by the Congregationalists, the Reformed peoples, the Baptists, the Amish, and some English Presbyterian groups—women have a great deal more stature under the Fatherhood of God (because they are all brothers and members of the priesthood of believers). At least the interaction within the church service differs, in that even in the early congregational meetings women were allowed to speak. Many women of this egalitarian tradition were among the early workers in the suffrage movement and many now are spokeswomen for the present liberation movement.

The third distinct religious variation in European denominations is that of the Celtic peoples, who occupied the fringe areas of Scotland, Wales, and Ireland. Since they are the original layer of habitation for the British Isles, the Celtic peoples—notably Scots and Welsh—retain many old traditional familial and tribal forms. It is the Celts who live scattered about in open farmsteads and keep cattle, whose religion is peopled by spirits and leprechauns as well as by God and the angels, and whose emphasis on family and clan gives the woman a pivotal place in kinship and lineage. Studies are now in progress of peoples living up and down the Appalachian and Ozark mountain chains and attached to the fringe of Southern and Midwestern towns under the label of "hillbillies."

Of course, after having been resettled on this continent for a hundred or two hundred years, most of the communal groups belonging to each culture area have modified themselves to adapt to new circumstances. Yet cultures are surprisingly persistent. We find Polish festivals in the streets of Chicago, St. Patrick's Day gatherings in Boston and New York. New England Congregationalist villages are repeated in Kansas and Oregon, still cooperating as "brothers" to celebrate the Fourth of July. Lloyd Warner[7] did an elegant study of one of these celebrations, Memorial Day, in a New England city in which the Puritans re-created their past in a parade of floats symbolically stating their values and world view.

My own "people" for ethnographic study have been the Scots Presbyterians who migrated into the Southern Piedmont in the eighteenth century. They are mixed Celtic and Anglo-Saxon, originating in the southwest of Scotland where the Covenanters were active. In their present-day summer community, gathered together for religious conferences and family reunions, the world view of Calvinistic Presbyterianism shouts out loud and clear. The aspect of this world view that pertains most directly to women is that of separation between the "flesh" and the "spirit." The "world" is associated with the city and with the worldly wickedness of drunkenness, sexual activity, gambling, and other licentiousness. The spiritual and good things can best be found in rural environments, in the old scattered open-country neighborhood of the ancestors and in the traditional sacred grove, where Celtic rituals were held in communication with the spirits of the forest. Women take the children at the beginning of the summer into this idyllic community in the mountains and set up housekeeping, the men visit at vacation times. The stated purpose is to give the children a safe place to spend the summers away from the environment of the city and to get together with the greater family. Unstated purposes are to have the children meet others of their own kind and later to marry a suitable person and bring the grandchildren back every summer to continue the cycle.

In this group, as in much of general American society, women are assigned those tasks in the home and in the church that are associated with the flesh and with the earth. Because they are tied to menstruation and childbearing they are presumably closer to the earth and to the flesh. Their tasks include cleaning of the house and food preparation, as well as handling of children's bodily needs such as diapering and bathing.

In addition, women make arrangements for the preparing of food for family reunions and for all activities honoring the dead ancestors. Men, meanwhile, read and study for the ministry, preach sermons, argue lawsuits, and read newspapers. Interestingly, the patterns of inheritance follow these grooves, with sons inheriting their fathers' law books and judicial robes, pulpit Bible or tools of the business trade. Girls inherit their mothers' jewelry, and the family silver and china passes down the line from mother to daughter.

The most obvious expression of dichotomy between flesh and spirit is the separation of girls and boys for many activities of play and learning. Among adults this separation is particularly noticeable when applied to married couples. There are no mixed social occasions which men and women attend apart from their spouses during the entire period of sexual activity—a period of around twenty-five years. During this time married women attend the Ladies' Bible Class, sing in the choir, go to the Garden Club, and devote their professional energies to rearing their children "in the nurture and admonition of the Lord." After these years, of course, they have to devote considerable energy to being available for the long summer visits of their grown daughters with all the grandchildren.

The kin network and the family unity are based on this mother-daughter tie. Closest of kin are the children born from one mother. (A half-brother or half-sister is a person who had the same father but different mother. All children born from one mother are full siblings whether they had different fathers or not.) This finding of the centrality of the mother-daughter bond is substantiated in the visiting patterns in which daughters bring children home to visit mother during the summer and in which the cousins who are the closest kin are the children of sisters because they always played together at grandmother's in the summer.

Careful examination and comparison of ethnographic data from the major subcultural groups in the United States reveals that there is a strong tendency in all of these to emphasize the centrality of the mother in transmitting the cultural heritage. This is pronounced in the Jewish family[8] and we hear a great many jokes about it, but it is apparent from the data that the central role of mother as socializer is shared by the major European traditions. It is within the kernel of the family unit that all the lore and laws of a people are learned. This kinship core becomes increasingly important in a people who live in scattered small-family bands and gather together only a few times a year. If each subculture is to survive as an entity, then the children must be taught the ways of the tribe and they must be brought together for the ceremonial times so the sacred interpretations of the universe can be passed on.

If the mother waltzes off to medical school or goes into business apart from the family or decides to accept a research grant to the University of Zambia, then how will the heritage persist? It is this pivotal role of mother as tradition maintainer within religious subcultures that makes the tightly knit groups resistant to social change in women's roles.

The internal segments within U.S. Christianity are equally a part of the not-so-humorous "chicken soup syndrome" that operates to keep married women—and especially mothers—in their proper place. Catholic schools crank out the slogan: "The man is head of the home, the woman is the heart." Protestants believe that "God couldn't be everywhere, so He made Mothers."

While church pastors and counselors continue to worry about the children of working mothers, no one has thought much about the startling statistic that 90 percent of all juvenile offenders have fathers who work.

It seems to me that the real structural problem to be cracked is that which allows only one role to the mother of a family. While in every tradition there seems to be a slot open for the spinster who chooses a career, there seems to be no acceptable slot for a woman with a family who pursues a career assertively. She does this against very real and very formidable negative social barriers. Allowing such a new role in a traditional culture would threaten the continuation of that culture.

Liberation

Anthropologists are always accused of being conservative or even reactionary, because they paint a dismal picture of the possibilities for social and cultural change. It is not my intention to be gloomy or to imply that these internal traditional groups are holding millions of women captive against their will. I simply intend to describe and define what I see as happening in the ethnographic sense.

Applied anthropologists have a history of going into a culture with their brushes and trowels, defining the contours, grooves or meanings, natural social groupings, and then attempting to implement programs that will in fact bring about change without destroying life ways and cultural arrangements.

I would like to think that a thorough understanding of religious-cultural learning of sex roles and of internal social groups could point us the way to a well-designed program for Liberation that would fit with cultural meanings and values.

Somehow, however, I am not optimistic about this as a possibility. World view *is* the explanation of the relation of the sexes to each other and to the natural world.

What I do see as a possibility is the emergence of a new cultural group composed of those who have in some way broken loose from the old ways and are trying to live newly structured liberated lives. Earlier, while toying with this social model, I tagged this group as "the maypole dancers." Another Lentz Lecturer, John Westerhoff, has developed this idea to postulate a new religion for these people.[9] The maypole dancers include the intelligentsia—the academics, intellectuals, seminary students, and others who have made a conscious choice to attempt to break out and live by new rules with new loyalties. (Sometimes there seem to be more of them than there are—the reason of course, being that *they* are the ones writing the sociology books!)

Because no human being can grow up outside a cultural group, the maypole dancers will have to invent new kin relationships, new rituals, new community forms within which to pass on their own world view of freedom and equality. Already we see these emerging in family-like communes, joint families, and informal marriages with "satellite" husbands or wives. We see new kinship gatherings when groups of families who have taught at the same university or lived in the same town re-establish friendship at holiday times in preference to visiting blood kin. We see local congregations, particularly in the Unitarian movement, where children and parents and older adults, formerly members of assorted denominations, are attempting to establish rituals that communicate new possibilities in restructuring sex and age roles. Networks of families within church congregations go out to state parks for weekend camping, where a tribal *communitas* has new rules. Liberated rules allow cross-sex friendships, nondefensive adolescent and adult confrontations, and a modified extended family. Young children can have the benefit of ten or twelve older adopted siblings to look after them, and older children can express wonder at new infants. In these new scattered-and-gathered communities children see daddies cooking and washing and mommies reading law books and writing lectures. They experience one-parent families who are a part of the total mosaic instead of some deviation from the norm. And, in a supportive community setting, when individuals fall back into older stereotyped behaviors it is safe to reprimand, to insist on changes and reparations without the danger of being labeled a weirdo or a freak.

Equality at the economic level is essential for women. Equal pay, time off for pregnancy, ability to establish credit and to own property are crucial to emancipation. Equality at the political level is also essential. Women must be able to vote and to hold office and must be represented in proportion to their numbers in the population. These goals must be pursued in conjunction, however, with the goals of liberation at the level of family and kin-religious interaction. Goals at this level would include the freeing of women and men from religious socialization practices that stereotype the contribution of either sex. When the church teaches that women must stay at home and follow the natural law of having babies and rearing them in the faith, it is implicitly teaching that men are harnessed to the work world as "providers." Then neither one is free.

As human beings we can never be free from cultural patterning and cultural persistency. As human beings we do have the cognitive tools to analyze and hopefully to change these invisible forces. Culture and learning have brought us as women into a position we are no longer willing to accept. *Liberation* is our word for creatively coming out of cultural shells into new possibilities.

NOTES

1. Hall, E. T. *The Silent Language.* Garden City, N.Y.: Doubleday, 1966.
2. Arensberg, C. M. and Solon T. Kimball. *Culture and Community.* New York: Harcourt Brace & World, 1965.
3. Chapple, Elliot D. and Carelton Coos. *Principles of Anthropology.* New York: Holt, Rinehart & Winston, 1942.
4. Turner, Victor. *The Ritual Process.* Chicago: Aldine, 1969.
5. Weisstein, Lenore J., *et al.* "Sex-Role Socialization in Picture Books for Pre-school Children." *American Journal of Sociology,* Vol. 77, Number 6, pp. 1125–1151.
6. Anderson, Charles. *White Protestant Americans.* Englewood Cliffs, N.J.: Prentice-Hall, 1970.
7. Warner, W. Lloyd. *The Family of God.* New Haven: Yale University Press Paperback, 1961.
8. Greenberg, Dan. *How to Be a Jewish Mother.* Los Angeles: Price, Stern, and Sloan, 1964.
9. Westerhoff, John. "Religious Education for the Maypole Dancers." Unpublished Lentz Lecture delivered at Harvard University, 1972.

JUDAEO-CHRISTIAN INFLUENCES ON FEMALE SEXUALITY

Dorothy D. Burlage

This essay is addressed to a particular audience—women and men who are influential or active in the Christian church, whether as members, ministers, religious leaders, educators, theological students, or Sunday-school teachers, and to those parents who are offering their children moral guidance based on church teachings about women and sexuality. If there were a dedication, it would be to those women who have experienced sexual shame, fear, or ignorance because of their strict religious training, for they are the ones whose suffering has inspired this article.

The influence of the Judaeo-Christian tradition on female sexual behavior is an immense and complicated topic for which this essay serves only as an introduction. The focus here is on contributions from social and behavioral science research, with the hope that the findings and conclusions of researchers will be so convincing as to provoke more intense attention to, and discussion of, these issues by church leaders, parents, and all women in the church.

Because of the brevity of this article, several of the most serious concerns related to female sexual behavior have been omitted rather than treated superficially or inadequately: the relationship between sexual repression and mental illness, the effects of sexual denial and the double standard on men, the changing functions of the family, and the constellation of interrelationships among the female role, the family, the church, and the state. These topics deserve serious consideration and exploration if female (and human) oppression and liberation are to be understood, for finally they are related to the basic issues of racism and violence, war and peace.

The topics addressed here include the biblical sources of the sexual oppression of women, its contribution to the double standard, and the sexual patterns of women who have been influenced by the Judaeo-Christian tradition. The article goes on to discuss how women are taught to be sexually repressed. It then catalogues some of the problems which can arise as a result of strict religious training, including sexual problems in marriage and religious influences on divorce, difficulties in pregnancy, childbirth, and nursing. Although these early portions assume the anti-sexual teachings of the church which has characterized it for hundreds of years, the final section will consider some of the recent changes in sexual behavior patterns and the ethical standards of the church.

Influential Judaeo-Christian Views of Women

It is important for women and men to take seriously what the Judaeo-Christian tradition says about women and sexuality because the church, as the "guardian of public morality," has been crucial in shaping sexual and social behavior in both civil and religious institutions. Religious influence is conveyed directly to young girls and to adult women through sermons, religious training, and Bible study. In addition, parents, trying to structure the moral standards of their children, look to religious authorities for sanction and guidance. The Judaeo-Christian tradition is the foundation of most of our civil laws governing marriage, divorce, and other sex-related behavior—abortion, contraceptive methods, pre- and extra-marital sexuality. Finally, the informal social norms in Western Civilization as well as its political and economic institutions reflect church teaching on the subject of women, so that in every fact of our social behavior the church has been a major influence on our values and roles.

Some scholars are giving careful attention to the role of women in the Bible and throughout church history. Some have documented the subservient roles of women in the patriarchal family patterns of the Old and New Testaments and the continued degrading of women in the history of the church.[1] Others are presenting a more complicated picture, highlighting the more positive views of women to be found in the Bible.[2] Regardless of where these investigations lead or how encouraging some of the recent research may be, it seems clear that the church has usually emphasized, and based its treatment of women on, those texts in the Bible which can be interpreted to inhibit and restrain female sexual behavior.

While attending church, small children and many adults listen to Bible readings without the benefit of scholarly exegeses and interpretations.[3] Consider what a young girl might hear about women in church and how that might contribute to her identity as a woman:

To the woman he said, "I will greatly multiply your pain in childbearing; in pain you shall bring forth children, yet your desire will be for your husband, and he shall rule over you." (Gen. 3:16)

You shall not covet your neighbor's house; you shall not covet your neighbor's wife, or his manservant, or his maidservant, or his ox, or his ass, or anything that is your neighbor's. (Exod. 20:17)
[Note the concept of property involved when "wife" is construed as parallel to "house," "field," "ox," "ass."]

If a man seduces a virgin who is not betrothed, and lies with her, he shall give the marriage present for her, and make her his wife. If her father utterly refuses to give her to him, he shall pay money equivalent to the marriage present for virgins. (Exod. 22:16–17)

And I find more bitter than death the woman, whose heart is snares and nets, and whose hands are fetters: whoso pleases God escapes from her; but the sinner is taken by her. (Eccles. 7:26)

Give not your strength to women, your ways to those who destroy kings. (Prov. 31:3)

[I desire] also that women should adorn themselves modestly and sensibly in seemly apparel, not with braided hair or gold or pearls or costly attire, but by good deeds, as befits women who profess religion. Let a woman learn in silence with all submissiveness. I permit no woman to teach or to have authority over men; she is to keep silent. For Adam was formed first, then Eve; and Adam was not deceived, but the woman was deceived and became a transgressor. Yet woman will be saved through bearing children, if she continues in faith and love and holiness, with modesty. (I Tim. 2:9–15)

Wives, be subject to your husbands, as to the Lord. For the husband is the head of the wife as Christ is the head of the church, his body, and is himself its Savior. As the church is subject to Christ, so let wives also be subject in everything to their husbands. (Eph. 5:22–24)

Although the sexual prohibitions have not been exclusively directed toward women, women seem to have suffered more than men for two reasons. First, the laws and exhortations regarding women are much stronger than those regarding the behavior of men, resulting in a double standard for men and women. Second, church membership lists suggest that more women than men are active church members, and it is likely that they are also more constantly and intensively subjected to religious teachings.

The major Biblical themes which the Church has emphasized in its moral teachings reflect the patriarchal family patterns of the Old Testament. Patriarchy had several implications: that men had exclusive rights to political, legal, and economic power; that inheritance should pass from father to son and property could not be owned by women; that the primary function of women was reproduction and the care of children, while men were given the economically productive roles.

In order to guarantee the legitimacy of the male heirs, the sexual behavior of women had to be circumscribed to relations with legal husbands (effective birth control was, of course, unknown); otherwise there would be arguments over the father's inheritance. Because women had no means of economic support except that of father or husband and no opportunity for independent earning, they needed husbands for financial support of themselves and their children. Any sexual activity on the part of women except in marriages would threaten the patriarchal system by endangering the patriarchal succession. In addition, historians of sexual behavior assert there is a direct relationship between the Judaic patriarchal family structure, the concept of women as property (see Exod. 22: 16 above), and the social acceptance of the double standard in Western culture. In this interpretation, adultery is not a violation of the woman, but of man's property rights.[4]

It is no surprise, then, that the female biblical characters who have received the most attention from the church and functioned as role models for women are defined by their sexual behavior: Eve, the temptress, and Mary, the virginal mother. The world of women was polarized into "nice" girls and "bad" girls, sexual women and asexual women.

The notion of woman as temptress or whore, responsible for the original sin and fall of man, was especially popular among the Church Fathers. Consider what Tertullian says about women:

You are the devil's gateway: You are the unsealer of that forbidden tree: You are the first deserter of the divine law: You are she who persuaded him whom the devil was not valiant enough to attack. You destroyed so easily God's image, man. On account of your desert—that is, death—even the Son of God has to die.[5]

Eve, now seen as representative of all women, is considered responsible not only for seducing man, but for the crucifixion of Jesus.

This view of woman, associating her with sin, sex, death, and the devil, was taken to its bizarre extremes by the church of the Middle Ages when it was responsible for murdering women accused of being "witches." Some scholars estimate the number of women who died because of this charge to be in the millions.[6] The crimes of which they were accused were sexual in content: rendering men impotent, castrating men, performing abortions, practicing birth control, and making men excessively passionate. An excerpt from the *Malleus Maleficarum*, the manual for witch hunters written by the Reverends Kramer and Sprenger (the "beloved sons" of Pope Innocent VIII) in 1484, summarizes the charges:

Now there are, as it is said in the Papal Bull, seven methods by which they infect with witchcraft the venereal act and the conception of the womb: First, by inclining the minds of men to inordinate passion; second, by obstructing their generative force; third, by removing the members accommodated to that act; fourth, by changing men into beasts by their magic act; fifth, by destroying the generative force in women; sixth, by procuring abortion; seventh, by offering children to the devils, besides other animals and fruits of the earth with which they work much harm. . . .[7]

If Eve was the female character who symbolized sin and sex, Mary was the prototype of virtue. Interpreted as the woman who could give birth to the Son of God without any sexual contact or experience, she has been the model to which women have been taught to aspire as wives and mothers. Many women, emulating Mary, have given primary importance to their reproductive and child-rearing functions in the family, with sexual expression limited to the purpose of procreation.

The biblical tradition imposes upon those who are Christian, both women and men, a single standard of sexual morality: total abstinence outside marriage. Notable among the references which have shaped traditional Christian sexual norms is the Hellenistic-influenced list of vices recorded in Mark 7:21–22; in addition to evil thoughts, theft, murder, pride, and foolishness, this list also includes fornication (traditionally interpreted as nonmarital intercourse), licentiousness (usually understood as inclination to sensuality or sexual excesses), and adultery. However, although the strict prohibitions against nonmarital sexual activity have been applied to men and women alike, they have had particularly harsh results for women.

In the cultural context out of which the Bible was written, women were primarily described by the categories of virgin, wife, widow, or slave; if they were not one of these, they most often held the identity of "harlot" or "adulteress." And according to biblical treatment of the female sex, no other identities were so despised in a woman. For example, in the Old Testament the marriage relationship provides one of the major images for describing the relationship between Israel and Yahweh. Beginning with the time of the Mosaic covenant, a major danger for the sons of Israel was that they would "play the harlot after [foreign] gods." (Exod. 34:16) When Israel as a people was unfaithful to the covenant, she was usually described as a "harlot." It is the sexual infidelity of women, not men, which carries sufficient moral disgrace as to furnish an apt image for Israel's unfaithfulness to Yahweh.

In the New Testament, harlots and tax collectors were considered the very worst elements of society. One indication of their status is Jesus' contrast between them, as those considered most "immoral," and the chief priests and elders, supposedly the righteous members of Jewish society, when he warned the latter that tax collectors and harlots would enter the Kingdom of God before those temple officials: "For John came to you in the way of righteousness, and you did not believe him, but the tax collectors and the harlots believed him." (Matt. 21:32)

The Biblical tradition has been less severe for men, especially in the Old Testament, where there are several examples of polygamy. The only sexual taboos for men in the Old Testament forbid masturbation, since that would result in the "wasting of semen," and prohibit adultery (defined as sexual relations with a *married* woman), since that would undermine the patriarchal family and the concept of wives as the property of their husbands. Yet the punishment of male adulterers could not compare with that inflicted on adulteresses.[8]

Because the Biblical tradition has had such different views of men's and women's roles and sexual behavior, it has provided an atmosphere which tacitly allowed the development of a double standard whereby women are punished more harshly for nonmarital sexual activity. Although violation of the "single standard" of abstinence from sexual relations outside marriage may induce feelings of guilt and failure in both men and women, such violation seems also to subject women to severe role and identity changes not experienced by men.

Other aspects of the Biblical tradition have added their burdens on women. Females are considered "unclean" because of the taboos about menstruation in the Old Testament.[9] The notion of women being unclean, combined with the negative references to nakedness in the Creation story, contribute to the shame and fear women feel about their bodies.

The Pauline texts of the New Testament not only add dimensions of discrimination against women, but also carry an anti-sex, anti-marriage message, suggesting that the devout will not marry at all but lead a celibate life. Some elements in the New Testament reflect another major element in church tradition: the separation of soma and psyche or body and spirit. This notion represented the influence of Hellenism on early Christian thought; nevertheless, it has had significant impact on subsequent Christian ideas of love and sexuality.

Although it is probably true that the church, in keeping with historical changes, has become more liberal, many young girls still are socialized to see sexuality only as an evil. Many are still taught to obey and submit to their husbands, to envisage their primary function as rearing children, and to think of themselves as inferior to men.

The Influence of Religious Belief on Female Sexual Patterns

Religious commitment effects considerable differences in female sexual behavior, just as the double standard contributes to the differences between male and female sexual activity. These differences have been most comprehensively documented in the studies of female and male sexual behavior conducted by Alfred Kinsey and his colleagues. The Kinsey research, which included a sample of 7,789 females and 8,603 males, looked at the effect of several factors on sexual behavior—among them age, education, occupation, geographic origin, and decade of birth. Kinsey included Protestants, Catholics, and Jews in his study, and divided each of these major faiths into "devout," "moderately devout," and "inactive."

Kinsey's findings revealed that of the many possible influences on women's sexual patterns, religion was the single most important. The degree of religious devotion was found in almost every respect to be more important than whether the particular commitment was to the Protestant, Catholic, or Jewish faith.

Kinsey studied several kinds of sexual behavior, including preadolescent sexual play among children, masturbation, premarital petting, premarital coitus, extramarital coitus, and homosexuality. He also considered the total sexual activity of women, and how religion affects their accumulated sexual experience. To understand specifically how religion has influenced sexual behavior, it is important to consider some of these patterns in more detail.

Kinsey found religion to be the most important factor in determining the frequency and number of total sexual outlets for women. This was true of both married and unmarried females, Catholic, Protestant, and Jewish, with the more devout having the least sexual expression and the least religiously active having the most sexual outlets.[10] Religion has had a similar effect on married women: "Religious backgrounds of the females in the sample had definitely and consistently affected their total outlet after marriage. In nearly every age group . . . small percentages of the more devout and larger percentages of the inactive groups had responded to orgasm after marriage."[11]

Regarding premarital petting, Kinsey says: "The chief restraint on petting and on petting which leads to orgasm seems to have been the religious restraint against it. . . . Because religious tradition has so strongly shaped public thinking on these matters, its restraining influence is apparent not only among those who are devout, but at least to some extent, among those who are not directly connected with any religious group."[12]

An interesting relationship is found between religious belief and masturbation: though it violates Old Testament teachings, masturbation provides a larger proportion of total sexual outlet for the more devout than the less devout. Kinsey hypothesizes that the devout rely more on masturbation as a sexual outlet because it may seem less sinful than premarital petting or coitus.[13]

Religious commitment and the decade in which the female is born are the major factors correlated with female premarital behavior. For example, 63 per cent of the religiously inactive unmarried Protestants had premarital coital experience, while less than half as many, or 30 per cent, of the devout Protestants had such experience.[14] Kinsey also asked about the emotional reactions of women who had engaged in premarital coitus and found religion the most important factor in whether a woman felt guilt and regret.[15]

Religion and educational levels are the factors most highly correlated with homosexual activity, according to Kinsey's study. Religious activity seemed to be a restraining factor in initiating homosexual contact. Some very devout women reported they had felt such a conflict because of the discrepancy between their religious code and their homosexual behavior that they had left the church.[16] Ironically, however, some of the females reported they had engaged in homosexual activity precisely because of the religious prohibitions against heterosexual activity.

As one might expect, religious belief was the most important variable in extramarital female behavior. As an example, among women in their early thirties, four times as many inactive Protestants as devout Protestants had extramarital relations.[17]

The cumulative premarital experience of a woman is the greatest predictor of her ability to have satisfaction in marital sexual relations. If a woman has had orgasm premaritally, whether in petting, dreams, masturbation, or coitus, then she is likely to have orgasm in marriage. If she has not had such premarital experience, she is less likely to have orgasm in marriage. Thirty-six per cent of the females in Kinsey's sample had married without having had previous experience in orgasm. Of this group, 44 per cent had failed to respond to the point of orgasm in the first year of marriage."[18] Premarital experience was more important than religion in predicting marital orgasmic potential although religion and premarital experience are themselves highly correlated. Kinsey found a significant difference between the more and the less devout Catholic women, with the devout including a higher percentage who completely failed to reach orgasm.[19]

In contrast to these patterns of female sexual behavior, the males were significantly less influenced by religion. Social factors, such as the male's educational and social levels, proved more important than religion in predicting sexual behavior. However, religiously devout men were less likely to engage in some sexual activities than men without religious commitment, and their frequency of engaging in such activity was less than that of the religiously inactive men.[20]

Kinsey's studies, in summary, give substantial evidence of the existence of the double standard and of the influence of religious moral codes on sexual behavior. In addition, his studies highlight how religious piety, by condemning some sexual behaviors more than others, is associated with the very sexual expressions it labels perversions—masturbation and homosexuality. Finally, he documents the way in which premarital restraint of sexual behavior is correlated with adult inhibitions in marital relations, although the church sanctions sexual expression in marriage.

Sexual Repression, Marriage, and Divorce

Some religious people may find the Kinsey data encouraging—the church is doing "the Lord's work" and the only problem is how to get the "strays back into the fold." They may interpret the sexual denial of devout women as an indication of their superior moral standards and self-discipline. Perhaps that is true, but given what social science tells us about how behavior is learned, it is much more likely that the sexual behavior of adults, and its denial, is not so much a question of adult "will power" as of childhood training that results in limited capacity for sexual expression and autonomous choice. The intent of the next sections of this essay is to explore how women learn sexual inhibitions and some of the effects of that repressive process.

Parents and educators, on the basis of common sense and experience, have always known that the training of the young is important in shaping adult values, attitudes, and behavior. To give obvious examples, this is the operating assumption when parents teach their children to brush their teeth and eat their spinach. The parental expectation is that these patterns will continue into adulthood.

The socialization of sexuality in children became the focus of scientific research about seventy-five years ago, when Sigmund Freud and other physicians began to study the relationship between physiological symptomology and emotional difficulties. Freud scandalized the Victorian world by writing openly about the sexual instincts of children and the neuroses and perversions which could result from the repression of such feelings. He claimed that sexual needs were innate, "instinctual," in all people, just like the needs to eat and sleep; if these needs were repressed, they could be partially sublimated into other activities but were likely to come out in distorted forms of psychosis and neurosis.

By interrupting the sexual development of children, extreme parental training can minimize or prevent altogether the capacity for healthy sexual expression. This theory of the socializing process of young girls offers another explanation of why Kinsey found that the greatest predictor of marital sexual satisfaction was the extent to which women had felt free to express themselves sexually in earlier years.

Since Freud's time, the socialization of children, sexuality, and personality development have been areas of research explored by psychologists and psychiatrists. Whereas most of that research was based on clinical evidence, Dr. William H. Masters and Mrs. Virginia E. Johnson made a major contribution in recent years with their laboratory studies of sexual functioning.[21] Masters and Johnson studied the sexual behavior of women and men under laboratory conditions and documented sexual dysfunctioning in their therapeutic treatment of the sexual problems of married couples.

Their research indicates that religious orthodoxy is a major predictor of female (and male) sexual inadequacy: "Religious orthodoxy still remains of major import in primary orgasmic dysfunctions as in almost every form of human sexual inadequacy."[22]

Masters and Johnson describe the way early childhood training makes sexual difficulties for adult women:

> Instead of being taught or allowed to value her sexual feelings in anticipation of appropriate and meaningful opportunity for expression, thereby developing a realistic sexual value system, she must attempt to repress or remove them from their natural context of environmental stimulation under the implication that they are bad, dirty, etc.[23]

Not only are women not allowed to develop their own values

regarding sexual behavior, but the sexual repression seems to be much greater in its effects than was even intended to meet social standards—"to maintain virginity, to restrain a partner's sexual demand, or even to conduct interpersonal relationships in a manner considered appropriate by representative social authority."[24]

Such women were exposed in their formative years to concepts such as "sex is dirty," "nice girls don't involve themselves," "sex is the man's privilege," and "sex is for reproduction only,"[25] the very concepts attributed to religious training and the biases of the double standard. According to Masters and Johnson, women raised with these values or simply ignorant of sexual matters face a crisis upon physiological maturity. At this point they can deal with repression in different ways—some develop unrealistic relationships, some look for gratification in other social activities, and some desperately search for substitute values. Depending on how this crisis is resolved, sexual dysfunctioning can become an "ongoing way of life."[26]

For some women, repression is handled gracefully until marriage, at which time they report that they don't feel anything in sexual relations, a condition known as "pelvic anesthesia." The combination of biophysical and psychosocial systems of influence has resulted in the inability of women to be sexually responsive to their husbands.

Masters and Johnson found religious orthodoxy to be a major etiological factor in vaginismus, a psychosomatic difficulty in which the pelvic musculature is so constricted as to make coital function impossible. Where vaginismus was diagnosed, the married partners had not been able to consummate the marriage:

Consider the case of one couple who came to Masters and Johnson for help:

> After nine years of a marriage that had not been consummated, Mr. and Mrs. A. were referred to the Foundation for treatment. . . . Mrs. A's family background was one of unquestioned obedience to parents and to disciplinary religious tenets. . . . Other than her father, religion was the overwhelming influence in her life. . . . The specific religious orientation, that of Protestant fundamentalism, encompassed total dedication to the concept that sex and sin were synonymous words. . . . There were long daily sessions of family prayer. . . . On Sunday the entire day was devoted to the Church, with activities running the gamut

of Sunday school, formal service, and young people's groups. . . . The day of her wedding, Mrs. A. was carefully instructed to remember that she now was committed to serve her husband. It would be her duty as a wife to allow her husband "privileges." She was told that "good women" never expressed interest in the "thing." Her reward for serving her husband would be, hopefully, in having children.[27]

The story goes on to describe how the woman's resistance to sexual contacts initiated by her husband was sufficiently successful so that after nine years of marriage she remained a virgin and the couple childless.

In another case of a woman suffering from vaginismus, the woman reported that she had grown up in a quite religious home where sexuality was never discussed except in terms of taboos. When the girl decided to marry, she received no advice from her family, but her religious advisor gave her some direction: "Coital connection was only to be endured if conception was desired."[28]

In one case, the problem was not only disabling to the woman herself, but resulted in her husband, also religiously orthodox, becoming impotent. She described her background as quite strict, dominated by "thou shalt not's."[29]

Sexual problems almost inevitably lead to emotional strain in a marriage. There can be a breakdown in communication, in openness, warmth and trust between the spouses. This discord can be one of the reasons for extramarital affairs, and sometimes results in the complete breakdown of the marriage. According to Kinsey, three-quarters of the divorces recorded in his studies included sexual problems among those difficulties which led to divorce.[30]

If religious training fosters those sexual problems which can lead to marital difficulty and even dissolution, it also affects patterns of divorce in other ways. Whereas the Old Testatment gave men more rights to divorce than women, the general position of the church has been its condemnation for either party and restrictions against remarriage. In fact, current divorce practice indicates not only the bias against divorce, but also the effects of the double standard.

In the most comprehensive survey to date of women who divorce, conducted by William J. Goode in 1948, religion was found to be a major factor in shaping divorce patterns. Goode found that the religious faith of women is correlated with divorce rates: Catholics are less likely to divorce than Protestants or Jews,[31] possibly because they fear excommunication. There was also a significant correlation between religious commitment, measured by church attendance, and divorce rates, with the frequent church attenders, both Protestant and Catholic, having a lower rate of divorce.[32] Reflecting the greater taboo against divorce in the Catholic church, the Catholics in Goode's sample were less likely to remarry than Protestants.[33]

Not only do church policy and religious commitment influence divorce patterns, but they seem to elicit feelings of guilt when the decision is made to divorce. Goode finds that women with religious affiliations feel their divorces reflect religious and moral failure, and consequently they feel guilt.[34] He also finds that Catholic women experience divorce as more "traumatic" than Protestant women.[35]

The double standard is operative in the different motivations that men and women have for initiating divorce. Both Goode and Kinsey find that women are much less likely to consider their husband's infidelity reason for divorce than men are ready to divorce their wives for the same reason. According to Kinsey's study, men "rate their wives' extramarital activities as prime factors in their divorces twice as often as the wives made such evaluations of their husband's activities."[36]

The Effects of Sexual Repression on Maternal Behavior

The fear and shame which some women experience about sexuality has repercussions not only in marital relations but also in their roles as mothers, particularly in pregnancy, childbirth, and nursing. Studies relating such anxiety to difficulties in the maternal role have not isolated religion as a variable, but have considered the effects of sexual inhibition and anxiety. Since sexual inhibition is often a reflection of religious teaching, it seems relevant to refer to the research.

Judith Bardwick, in her book *Psychology of Women,*[37] points out that amenorrhea (the suppression of menstruation for extended periods of time) can be used as a mechanism to avoid adult sexuality and conception and therefore "ameliorate sex anxiety."[38] She suggests that when the sexual aspects of women's relationships with men grow more important and there is a concomitant increase in sexual anxiety, women also exhibit an increase in psychosomatic symptoms. In a review of several studies on difficulties in pregnancy, such as excessive vomiting or excessive weight gain, Bardwick finds anxiety about sexuality one of the variables related to these complaints.[39]

The ability to breast-feed one's children also seems related to the mother's attitudes about sexuality, according to a study by Niles and Michael Newton.[40] In their review of studies on breast-feeding, they report on research done by Newson and Newson showing that "feelings of aversion for the breast-feeding act appear to be related to dislike of nudity and sexuality."[41] In a study by Salber and associates on women who have not tried to nurse, the researchers explain that "they were excessively embarrassed at the idea or too modest to nurse."[42] Other research has related the inability to nurse to sexual disturbances and to intolerance toward masturbation and social sex play by children.[43]

These studies are significant because they suggest that the prenatal period and early months of an infant's life (months that are critical to the child's development) may be affected by the sexual anxiety and inhibitions of the mother.

Major Changes in Sexual Behavior Patterns and Ethical Standards of the Churches

Both Kinsey's work and Ira Reiss' study of premarital behavior in America document the relationship between the double standard and prostitution.[44] The double standard assumes that men need, and should be allowed, sexual activity before marriage, but that women should be virginal until marriage. At the same time, married women are not allowed to have sexual relations except in marriage. These contradictory conditions necessitated the creation of an outlet for unmarried men, and thus fostered the institution of prostitution.

Since 1920 there has been a shift away from prostitution. After that year, an increasing number of women engaged in intense premarital sexual activity, including coitus, not for pay but for their own satisfaction.[45] It was this new trend which originally earned the title of "sexual revolution." "Religious" as well as "secular" people have been included among those who no longer live by the norms of the past, but who are developing new patterns of behavior.

Some persons have tried to maintain traditional standards, in revised form. Harvey Cox has described in *The Secular City* what some young women go through to retain the virginity demanded by their religious upbringing; they cultivate a split in personality and behavior so they can engage in extensive petting and still remain "technical virgins."[46]

Many other Christians, both men and women, have permitted themselves to engage in nonmarital coitus. Some of them have consequently been subject to feelings of guilt and failure about violating the New Testament standard of nonmarital abstinence. In addition, Christian *women* in this group are subject to a potential shift in identity: they fear they will be seen as promiscuous or as whores, classified among the lowest of the low—since the Biblical tradition offers only such negative labels to a woman who is sexually active but unmarried. As Cox points out in his discussion of the "technically fallen woman,"[47] she often experiences strong feelings of self-condemnation; she also faces potential exclusion from the community of her church, especially should her sexual activity lead to unwed pregnancy.

If religious teachings have typically restrained women from nonmarital sexual relationships, these teachings are also reported to be related to the development of the "swinging scene." "Swinging" is defined by its participants as wife-swapping, husband-swapping, and group sex, and in 1969 was estimated to include 45,000 American couples. In a study of the participants, described in *The Sex Researchers,*[48] Lynn and James Smith found that 50 per cent were raised as Protestants, 20 per cent as Catholics, and 7 per cent Jewish; the remainder belonged to minor faiths or had no religious affiliation.[49]

Many of the "swingers" explained their participation by their desire to overcome their strict religious upbringing and the sexual inhibitions they learned from their parents.[50] For example, one Protestant woman gave as her motive for swinging the "desire to be freed from her Puritan heritage."[51] A woman raised in a Catholic home and educated in Catholic schools explained that she had gotten into swinging to overcome her fear and inhibitions about sex.[52] Many women, after swinging, report not only a decrease in guilt and fear, but also increased self-esteem, self-confidence, and self-respect—results corroborating studies which have shown a correlation between self-esteem and sexual fulfillment.[53]

In contrast with those church-related persons who seek to maintain "technical virginity," become a "swinger," or who are overwhelmed by feelings of guilt and negative self-image, some churches and their members seem to be moving toward a more wholesome appreciation of sexuality for all humans, women as well as men. For example, female theologians and Biblical scholars are re-examining the Biblical sources of bias against women. Some male theologians have outlined new ethical positions on Christian sexual behavior. Some denominations are examining sex-role stereotypes and sex-specific language.[54] Some churches and religious schools have begun to offer sex education classes for both young people and adults.

One of the most significant recent investigations of these issues is a study on "Sexuality and the Human Community" sponsored by the Council of Church and Society of the United Presbyterian Church. This three-year study, completed in 1970, was carried out by a Task Force composed of clergy, social scientists, psychologists, theologians, and lay persons; it offers a serious, comprehensive, and courageous examination of sexual issues.

In some areas the Task Force study takes unusually advanced positions. For example, it suggests that the appropriate church and family attitude toward masturbation should free the experience of guilt and shame.[55] It offers the notion that though marriage and the family may have primacy as the pattern of heterosexual relationships, the fact that many church members are divorced, widowed, or intentionally single, suggests that the church should consider new ethical guidance which does not assume the procreative nuclear family for this large portion of church members.[56] In this regard, the report suggests: "Sexual expression with the goal of developing a caring relationship is an important aspect of personal existence and cannot be confined to the married and the about-to-be married."[57]

The spirit of inquiry in this study is admirable: a concern with the quality of human life and interpersonal relationships rather than simple rules of right and wrong; a willingness to utilize the insights about human behavior of the social sciences, especially psychology and psychiatry; a realization that the nuclear, patriarchal family is not a pattern common to many Christians outside the United States; and understanding that the American family as traditionally constituted is in a state of rapid change, and new forms such as communal living deserve consideration. It goes so far as to suggest that the church attend to the "Christian calling to glorify God by the joyful celebration of and delight in our sexuality. The attempts by some theologians to encourage Christians to appreciate the fact that our sexuality can be fun as well as functional has thrown some of our fellow faithful into paroxysms of fear and guilt."[58]

On some issues, the Task Force study seems unnecessarily equivocal or timid. Moreover, the General Assembly, the national ruling body of the United Presbyterian Church, voted at its annual meeting in 1970 to receive and distribute as a study document, but not to endorse, the Task Force findings. Nevertheless this study, in addition to the other liberal trends cited above, is a substantive beginning, hopefully to be expanded by further study and greater participation of the larger church membership.

Conclusion

The church professes a gospel of love, and yet it has perpetuated attitudes and behaviors inimical to that gospel. It has made physical and emotional intimacy a frightening experience rather than a natural one. It has taught fear, hate, and shame for the bodies which the Lord created and called "good." Where the New Testament spoke of the unity in Christ in which there is "neither male nor female," the church has not only contributed to the alienation and separation of the two, but considered the female a lesser being. And where the early church spoke of the old laws being transcended by the law of love, the church has used the old tradition to circumscribe women's freedom.

A major question for this writer is why the church has tended to be so vehement in maintaining its oppressive position on sexuality, particularly for women, when it more readily has altered and reinterpreted other aspects of the Biblical tradition. A good example is offered in the Presbyterian Task Force study: "We would find it intolerable . . . to base our treatment of fornication on the death penalties imposed in Deuteronomy 22 or to exclude eunuchs and bastards from 'the assembly of the Lord,' as prescribed in Deuteronomy 23."[59]

On other moral problems, the church has tended to be less literal in its interpretation of Biblical teaching. At best, in its frequent sanction of war and segregation, it has been ambivalent about the commandments to love your neighbor and not to kill. The insistence on strict literalism regarding sexual issues raises the question of why sin is so readily equated with sensuality and often taken so much more seriously than other "sins" or injustices. One suspects a deep fear of self-defined and self-controlled sexual expression, as well as the possible loss of moral authority over its members. Whatever the reasons for these tendencies in the church, the conclusion of the Canadian Council of Churches, in its study of sexuality in the Scriptures, seems germane: "Scripture alone provides an inadequate basis on which to construct a specific sexual morality for today."[60]

Another fundamental question is why the discrimination against women in the church has been accepted and perpetuated by its own women members. Perhaps men have had something to gain by the church's views of women. One can hypothesize that male religious leaders have wanted to protect their own status and power in the church, as well as be in a position to control the sexual behavior of women. Perhaps economic motives are also operative, as women have certainly provided much donated labor in the service of the church. A more extreme example of the economic issue is the Swedish law, on the books until 1915, which extracted a fine of two silver dollars from any woman who engaged in premarital sexual relations. It deserves notice that the money went into a fund to maintain church property.[61]

If women have been faithful to a religion which is so often demeaning to them, the obvious explanation is that the church was the major institution for the last several hundred years which welcomed women at all. If denied possibilities for economic self-sufficiency, and refused political and legal rights, women were at least allowed inside the door of the church and praised for their church suppers, sewing circles, and for teaching in parochial and Sunday schools.

Not only have women been active members of the church, but they have adhered to its rigid morality and raised their daughters accordingly. Obedience to a higher moral authority is probably only one of the reasons women have done so, for there were many economic and social realities which mothers understood only too well. One can sympathize with the maternal wish to protect daughters from social disapprobation, to help them keep the virginity which has been the ticket to a "good" marriage and the economic security otherwise unavailable to women. Where illegitimacy represented the denial of economic, legal, and social rights, one can sympathize with mothers' concern for marital as versus nonmarital sexual activity. And one can sympathize with mothers who do not want to see their daughters treated as "sexual objects" by men. These concerns are based in the realities of a patriarchal society and the double standard.

It is quite unlikely that mothers intended, when they gave admonitions such as "sex is dirty" and "nice people don't talk about such things," to contribute to their daughters' marital problems or their fear and embarrassment about maternal functions, much less to set the stage for rebellious "swinging" or "technical virginity." But because women have been too modest and "ladylike" to discuss sexual matters openly, and to become informed by scholarly research on the subject, they have all too often operated in ignorance. Moreover, women have been taught to think of the popularized Judaeo-Christian version of women as part of a divine and immutable plan, and therefore have not been open to other views of female sexual behavior.

With the role of women and family patterns changing in fundamental ways, it is essential that the church, especially its woman members, reconsider the church's teaching about women and begin to focus on changing the opportunities for women. Attention should be given to offering the next generations of women more control over their own lives—in the church as well as economically, legally, and sexually. We would suggest that every woman should have the right to sexual education; to knowledge of and comfort with her own body; the right to decide whether to have children, and, if so, when and how many; whether and how long she wants to be married; when and whether to have physical intimacy with another person.

If women are to have these rights, and the emotional and physiological capacity to exercise choice in expressing their sexuality, the church must examine not only the roles by which women have traditionally been defined but also how it influences the sexual development of young girls and women. It is not an easy task for the church to move from the traditionally puritanical view of women and sexuality to a more positive understanding of what it should teach regarding sexual expression. The confusion about sexual freedom versus sexual license is a problem for the irreligious as well as the religious, for scientists as well as ethicists.

Certain trends in the society reinforce the conviction of some church members that sexual freedom inevitably leads to sexual abuse or exploitation, partly because the words "freedom" and "license" are often used to confound rather than to clarify sexual issues. The development of Playboy clubs and the use of sexual images in mass media advertising, both of which try to convey a message of liberation and superior sexual freedom, are examples of such confusion; for, in actuality, they serve to commercialize and cheapen human relationships. Compulsive, superficial, and frustrating pseudo-sexuality is not freedom, but another trap in disguise.

Central to this dilemma of sexual freedom versus sexual license for the church is its contradictory assumptions about human nature. The church both reflects and instills a social paradox in its view of children. They are innocent babes, and should be kept innocent forever. On the other hand, they are innately sinful and will inevitably err in their ways. Given this set of assumptions, the only solution possible is oppressive rules which lead to repression.[62]

Scientific research on the growth process from infancy to adulthood can offer assistance in getting out of this dilemma. Knowledge about sexual and emotional development suggests that the emphasis on the "shall" and "shall not" of adult sexual activities is misleading; the more informed perspective would focus on the problem of raising sexually and emotionally healthy children. Clinical and laboratory studies of sexual problems are sufficient to help alleviate some of the fears and myths about sexuality. Research has produced considerable evidence, exemplified in small portion by the Kinsey and Masters and Johnson material cited above, to show that frustrated sexual development and repression in childhood and adolescence contribute to subsequent distortions and abuse of sexual feelings.

Future progress in the church on the issues of sex roles and sexual behavior demands courage and honesty about its hopes and fears for human relationships, as well as the kind of serious research and study recommended by the Presbyterian General Assembly.[63] The familial and economic relations of the Hebrews millennia ago and of the Church Fathers in the intervening several hundred years should no longer be seen as sufficient patterns by which to define present sex roles and moral standards. The fundamental question for the church is how completely and seriously it will interpret its message of love, for women as well as men: will it continue to use fear, guilt, and ignorance to minimize the natural human capacity for love, or will it include physical affection and its tender expression as part of the fullness of life proclaimed by Christ?

NOTES

1. For further exploration of the anti-female and patriarchal themes in the Bible, see Mary Daly, *The Church and the Second Sex* (New York: Harper & Row, 1968) and Sister Albertus Magnus McGrath, *What a Modern Catholic Believes About Women* (Chicago: Thomas More Press, 1972).
2. An example of recent scholarship which argues against a strictly patriarchal interpretation of the Old Testament can be found in an article by Phyllis Trible, "Depatriarchalizing in Biblical Interpretation," *Journal of the American Academy of Religion* XLI, No. 1 (1973), pp. 30–38.
3. For further development of the biblical views of sexuality, see Canadian Council of Churches, "The Biblical and Theological Understanding of Sexuality and Family Life," *Report of a Study of the Faith and Order Commission of the Canadian Council of Churches* (Toronto: The Ecumenical Institute of Canada, 1969).
4. Alfred C. Kinsey, *et al. Sexual Behavior in the Human Female* (New York: Pocket Books, 1953), pp. 322–323.
5. Ira L. Reiss, *Premarital Sexual Standards in America* (New York: The Free Press, 1960), p. 51.
6. Barbara Ehrenreich and Deirdre English, *Witches, Midwives, and Nurses: A History of Women Healers* (Oyster Bay, New York: Glass Mountain Pamphlets, no date), pp. 6–7.
7. *Ibid.*, p. 9.
8. For more extensive treatment of the differential treatment of male and female adultery, see the article by Gail Shulman, "View from the Back of the Synagogue," in this volume.

9. The taboo of "uncleanness" is discussed in depth in Shulman, "View from the Back of the Synagogue."
10. Kinsey, *Female Sexual Behavior*, pp. 521–522. For example, 34 per cent of the unmarried devout Catholic women experienced some orgasm, compared to 70 per cent of the inactive Catholics.
11. *Ibid.*, p. 529.
12. *Ibid.*, p. 247.
13. *Ibid.*, pp. 157–158.
14. *Ibid.*, p. 304.
15. *Ibid.*, pp. 318–319. For example, 35 per cent of devout Catholics regretted premarital sexual experience, but only 9 per cent of the inactive Catholics expressed regret.
16. *Ibid.*, p. 465.
17. *Ibid.*, p. 424.
18. *Ibid.*, p. 385.
19. *Ibid.*, pp. 381–382.
20. *Ibid.*, pp. 685–687.
21. William H. Masters and Virginia E. Johnson, *Human Sexual Response* (Boston: Little, Brown and Company, 1966); *Human Sexual Inadequacy* (Boston: Little, Brown and Company, 1970).
22. Masters and Johnson, *Human Sexual Inadequacy*, pp. 229–230.
23. *Ibid.*, pp. 215–216.
24. *Ibid.*, p. 223.
25. *Ibid.*, p. 225.
26. *Ibid.*, pp. 223–224.
27. *Ibid.*, pp. 230–233.
28. *Ibid.*, p. 254.
29. *Ibid.*, pp. 255–256.
30. Kinsey, *Female Sexual Behavior*, p. 12.
31. William J. Goode, *Women in Divorce* (New York: The Free Press, 1965), p. 35.
32. *Ibid.*, p. 37.
33. *Ibid.*, p. 278.
34. *Ibid.*, p. 10, p. 15.
35. *Ibid.*, p. 190.
36. Kinsey, *Female Sexual Behavior*, p. 436.
37. Judith M. Bardwick, *Psychology of Women: A Study of Biocultural Conflicts* (New York: Harper & Row, 1971).
38. *Ibid.*, p. 77.
39. *Ibid.*, p. 78.
40. Niles Newton and Michael Newton, "Psychologic Aspects of Lactation," in Judith M. Bardwick, ed., *Readings on the Psychology of*

Women (New York: Harper & Row, 1972), p. 278.
41. *Ibid.*
42. *Ibid.*
43. *Ibid.*
44. Kinsey, *Female Sexual Behavior*, pp. 322–323, and Reiss, *Premarital Sexual Standards*, pp. 98–99.
45. For elaboration of this change in sexual patterns, see Reiss, *Premarital Sexual Standards*, pp. 227–235, and Kinsey, *Female Sexual Behavior*, pp. 298–302.
46. Harvey Cox, *The Secular City: Secularization and Urbanization in Theological Perspective* (New York: Macmillan, 1965), p. 210.
47. *Ibid.*, p. 212.
48. Edward M. Brecher, *The Sex Researchers* (New York: The New American Library, 1971).
49. *Ibid.*, p. 292.
50. *Ibid.*, pp. 294–295.
51. *Ibid.*, p. 295.
52. *Ibid.*, p. 294.
53. *Ibid.*, p. 298.
54. For example, the New York Conference (Methodist) Task Force on the Status of Women in the Church recently prepared a preliminary report on "Sex Role Stereotyping in the United Methodist Nursery Curriculum" (mimeograph, n.d.). In 1973 the General Assembly of the United Presbyterian Church authorized a study of their *Worshipbook* which is to make an inventory of specific uses of sex-specific language and to recommend changes.
55. General Assembly of the United Presbyterian Church in the United States of America, *Sexuality and the Human Community* (Philadelphia: Office of the General Assembly, UPUSA, 1970), p. 15.
56. *Ibid.*, p. 35.
57. *Ibid.*, p. 36.
58. *Ibid.*, p. 8.
59. *Ibid.*, p. 9.
60. As quoted in *Sexuality and the Human Community*, p. 45.
61. Birgetta Linnér, "What Does Equality Between the Sexes Imply?" in Helen Wortis and Clara Rabinowitz, eds., *The Women's Movement* (New York: Holsted Press, 1972), p. 54.
62. Credit for the clarity of this insight is due Dr. John M. Shlien, Professor of Education and Counseling Psychology, Harvard University.
63. *Sexuality and the Human Community*, pp. 48–56.

ENRICHMENT OR THREAT? WHEN THE EVES COME MARCHING IN

Krister Stendahl

I feel quite awkward when asked to bring a male perspective to these essays that aim at a righting of the relation between women and men in the church, and especially when asked to speak honestly about the threat to us men. I doubt that I am the right person for this assignment, because it all seems so simple and obvious to me. Even the question of "enrichment or threat" strikes me as secondary. The first question is the one of justice and equality. That is the obvious one, without qualification or contingencies. Basic justice is simple. It is right.

I am less convinced about an approach that takes its point of departure from the definition of male and female characteristics. I am too uncertain about such definitions. I know too many exceptions on both sides of the sex barrier. I am not even quite so sure as many seem to be that the world or the church would automatically become much better or more peaceful if women were involved at all levels of decision-making, and so on. It is my guess that such would be the result, but I cannot bring myself to make such a projection the basis for my reasoning. I feel far more comfortable and honest in saying that the issue is primarily one of justice and equal opportunity. Even if some people tell me that the world and the church would suffer from the consequences of such equality, I say gladly: "So let us suffer together and pay the price of a fuller equality." I think the issue is that simple.

As to the potential threat, I would also like to relate that question to the matter of justice, and to a very specific kind of fear. For is it not true that where there is no justice, there is always fear? As I become increasingly aware of how I profit from habits and structures of culture that deep down I know not to be just, I become afraid. I think that such fear is the crucial issue as our society becomes aware of the oppression, suppression, and repression of persons and groups. In the matter of sexism—as in the matter of the Third World—such fear is, or will become, the more intense since we cannot even minimize or handle it paternalistically by speaking of oppressed *minorities*.

So, rather than speaking about the potential threat, we should bring into focus that fear which lurks overtly or covertly in the minds of those who profit from a system of privilege which they know deep down to be unjust. That fear is not a sign of a sensitive conscience, it is more self-serving. It is grounded in the awareness that it will not be possible to retain the privilege without force and violence—this also when the Eves come marching in.

Fear makes human beings ugly. Persons, groups, and institutions can be beautiful—in spite of original sin and the fall. But when seized by fear, human beings become ugly. Most evil in this world grows out of fear. And fear grows out of having what one knows one has no just right to have. When the Scriptures say that ". . . love casts out fear. For fear has to do with punishment. . ." (1 John 4:18), then I remember the Jewish story about the enthusiastic disciple who said to his rabbi that he loved him, and the rabbi asked him: "Do you know what hurts me?" When the disciple said, "No," the rabbi said: "If you do not know what hurts me, how can you say that you love me?" And if we turned that story around and had the dependent disciple reminding the rabbi of that insight, then it would fit our situation even better.

So there can be no enrichment without justice, and the fear of justice will obstruct our way toward the future. It is as simple as that. That is the analysis, the pattern within which I believe it possible to move beyond personal and institutional sexism in church and society. The rest is commentary, or even footnotes, relating specifically to the situation of the churches.

1. The emphasis on justice is a necessary one, especially in the churches and in theology, and that for a peculiar reason. The church wants to speak in distinctly Christian terms. But justice and the concern for justice is universal, a common, human urge. That

may be the reason why questions of plain justice have had difficulty in becoming Item Number One on the church's agenda. It does not sound "Christian enough." So Christian theologians have lost themselves in often penetrating and sometimes perverse reflection on distinction and polarity and subordination when it came to male and female. And simple calls for justice and equality were branded with the damaging designation "secular" or "worldly" or "political." The call for justice first is a call for first things first.

2. We need not document the fact that the church *de facto* is a bastion of male domination. To some this would seem especially true about the Roman Catholic Church; but one could argue that, in its own strange ways, the Roman Catholic Church has found ways of offering alternatives to the pervasive Protestant model of women as being confined to the sphere of kitchen and children. There are the saints, the only order in the church with a decent representation of women. (I guess because it is the only position in the church where quality was the only qualification.)

But there is little point in arguing about relative differences. The total record is not good. It is actually so bad that we must ask radical questions about whether both Scriptures and the Tradition of the Church do not constitute an ever-available force toward the perpetuated bondage of women in subordination. Judged by the actual history of interpretation and practice, that is certainly the case; and to an extent that does not allow us simply to blame the situation on the fact that the interpretation has been in the hands of self-serving males. (Which leads me to think of the problem before us as a deeply theological problem, *i.e.*, a problem that cannot be solved by isolated passages and traditions or by isolated updatings of history by confessing the sins of earlier generations.)

3. The question is theological in the sense that we must ask how it came about that the bursts of insights as to the image of God being both male and female (Gen. 1:27), and as to the subordination of woman being a sinful sign of the fall (Gen. 3:16), and about the overcoming somehow of that fall in Christ in whom there "is not male and female" (Gal. 3:28)—how those bursts of insight got lost and subordinated to the point that they were inoperative in the life and experience of the church and in the creative thinking of theologians.

I believe that a new point of departure from these and similar insights is called for in order to counteract a mere use of the biblical material, and especially the New Testament pictures of early Christianity, as a model for Christian existence and the life of the church. God does not want us to play first-century Bible Land together. He wants us to be where he has placed us, right here and now.

Which leads me to take more seriously than many do the habits of language, and especially the ways we speak—and hence tend to think—about God. All good theologians have always been in tune with that story about the person who came back from heaven and told what God looked like, saying: She is black. The masculinity of God, and of God-language is a cultural and linguistic accident, and I think one should also argue that the masculinity of the Christ is of the same order. To be sure, Jesus Christ was a male, but that may be no more significant to his being than the fact that presumably his eyes were brown. Incarnation is a great thing. But it strikes me as odd to argue that when the Word became flesh, it was to re-enforce male superiority.

Much so-called liberal theology has a special problem here, for it has tended to increase the anthropomorphism of Christian language. In moving away from the deeper aspects of trinitarian speculation, it centered more and more on the idea of God as the Father and made the imagery of Fatherhood the overarching metaphor for God. One started with the idea of "Father" and blew it up into divine proportions. The old process was reversed: Instead of saying that the One who created the world and nurtured the galaxies could even be called "Father" by the mystery of faith, anthropomorphism won out and the Father image became supreme. A metaphor of faith, with a specific and limited intention, hardened into a concept that was not checked by genuine transcendence, and it became trivialized. The time has come to liberate our thoughts of God from such sexism; and a richer trinitarian speculation with the Spirit (which happens to be female in Hebrew) may be one way toward that goal. It is obvious that those who say "God" and mean it cannot accept a male God without falling into idolatry.

4. Such attempts at rethinking and re-experiencing call for a critique and renewal of the traditional language of theology and liturgy and everyday life. For that reason, I take the matter of pronouns seriously. To many, such concerns seem trivial or ridic-

ulous. They are not. Language is powerful. Generic "man" is a real obstacle to the digested understanding and feeling of "male and female created he them." *He/She* is awkward in catalogues and prose, and perhaps we will get used to the use of plural style instead. *Freshperson* sounds awkward, but is not more awkward than *freshman* when one thinks about it. *Ms.* strikes me as artificial, but it is worth the point it makes; and we may soon come, anyway, to the point when we can speak and write to and of persons without *Mr.* and *Miss* and *Mrs.* Just as, I guess, we are slowly getting rid of the term *co-ed* for women students—a strange remnant of male society's language.

But the important thing is that language is a powerful means in the necessary and deadly serious task of consciousness-raising.

5. The fear and threat is often submerged among those of us who like to learn better ways as fast as possible; but, while speaking about language, I cannot refrain from saying something about the joke and the snickering tone that often accompany our talking about Women's Liberation. That's where the fears surface. Half seriously and half jokingly, the humor serves as a cover for the ambiguity of feelings. That's why the joke and the snickering deserve watching. There are jokes and jokes. (It is like dirty jokes. Some are funnier than dirty and some are dirtier than funny.) Such distinctions help. But there are times when even funny jokes are not funny any more—at least until the time when justice and equality allow us sufficient distance to enjoy them again. In the realm of sexism that time is pretty far off.

6. Then there is "When I Am Tired." On the high level of discussing justice and fears as we did in the beginning of this essay, it all appears both simple and beautiful . . . and it is. Even from a male perspective it is both simple and beautiful, for I know that my fears are wrong. But when I am tired the old Adam of Genesis Chapter Three longs to be back to a dream, reinforced by long practice. Then it would feel good if I could live in a world where my wife has had her beauty sleep and is totally bent on taking care of the tired pieces that stumble home from the office. Then it seems heaven to be protected and looked after. And why do I want to hear what she has done during the day, but hate to rehearse my own activities? And why is it that somehow I get upset—even worse, just plain irritated—if my wife is sick, but I take for granted

that when I am ill, she should love me even more and care for my every whim?

So I guess it is when we are tired that we are most ourselves. And I guess the need for help and care is not wrong. But the expectation of one-way traffic is. The perpetuation of stereotyped roles implicit therein is at the root of the problem.

7. In speaking of justice and equality, it is important to avoid new types of stereotyping. Efforts at Women's Liberation are sometimes criticized for casting the examples and the concerns in upper-middle-class terms. As if there were not many women who —if they and their families could afford it—would not love to leave their work and spend all their time in the home. And there are husbands who would be excellent homemakers while their wives assumed the role of primary breadwinners. So justice and equality really mean equal freedom of choice. Families with the urge to experiment with that freedom and with new tentative life-styles growing out of such experiments also beyond the nuclear family need support, and I would expect the churches to function as supportive in such ventures. The potential of the church is considerable in this area for the very reason that it seems to many to be an unlikely ally. For they see the church as the primary guardian of a stereotyped nuclear family with the good wife as homemaker plus unpaid volunteer. When the church becomes the support system in new family life-styles, it has a good chance of changing the climate in society.

There remain, of course, the financial inequities, with "double income" for families where both parents choose to work for pay or, rather, the inequity and hence lack of freedom of choice for those families in which one of the parents desires to be at home. But such inequities can be solved by taxation. In my native country of Sweden there is little financial gain in two full professional salaries as compared with one; hence, the choice of remunerative work or not is based more on interest and personal fulfillment rather than on economic grounds. Thereby the freedom of choice becomes more real.

Enrichment or threat? My reflections from a male perspective may not have been too helpful. In the name of justice, I am so simplistically sure that here is enrichment—or even necessity beyond the question of gain and loss. And as to the threat, I think

I understand it, but I am too old to feel it fully. By now I have lived most of my life and all of it as a male in a male-oriented society—and in the church, where it has been more fun than threatening to encourage the first steps toward ordination of women to the ministry. But I know of no job or position that I ever thought or dreamt of where I would have been in competition with a woman. So you can see why I feel awkward in speaking about the threat. I am too old and too steeped in my paternalism and condescension. I know that I feel too much on top of the situation, trying to be wise and generous while staying in command. And I do know that I am among the last of that breed.

I like to think that I am ready to see a new order. However, I cannot envisage it. Others will have to work out the enrichment and overcome the fear. I believe it will be a better order, since it promises to deliver us men from some of the fears that now cripple us in our true humanity and deprives the church and society of fullness in the image of God—male and female without the shackles of subordination but with the joys of being God's children. Thus sexism and faith are mutually exclusive. They really are! And we are at the point in the history of the church when we are given a better chance to overcome that form of slavery than any earlier period has had. What a chance and what a challenge!

THEOLOGY AFTER THE DEMISE OF GOD THE FATHER:

A Call for the Castration of Sexist Religion

Mary Daly

The basic presuppositions of this paper have been proposed in some detail in my book *The Church and the Second Sex,* published some four years ago, and more recently and far more radically in a number of articles.[1] I shall briefly review some of these before proceeding to the basic work of this paper, which is to explore the potential of the women's revolution for transforming what I shall, for the time being, call theological consciousness.

Basic to the work at hand is my conviction that there exists a worldwide sexual caste system involving birth-ascribed hierarchically-ordered groups and that this system is masked by sex-role segregation, which is harder to perceive than spatial segregation, as in a ghetto. This caste system is also masked by women's duality of status, for women have a derivative status stemming from relationships with men which tends to hide our infrahuman condition *as women.* Finally, this caste system is hidden by ideologies and institutions that alienate us as women from our true selves, deluding us with false identifications, sapping our energies, deflecting our anger and our hope.

Patriarchal religion has made it more difficult to see through the injustices of the system by legitimating and reinforcing it. The long history of legitimation of sexism by Christianity is by now too well known to require detailed repetition here. I need not allude to the misogynism of the Church Fathers—for example, Tertullian, who informed women in general: "You are the devil's gateway," or Augustine, who opined that women are not made in the image of God. I omit reference to Thomas Aquinas and his numerous commentators and disciples who defined women as misbegotten males. I pass over Karl Barth's proclamation that woman is ontologically subordinate to man and Dietrich Bonhoeffer's insistence that women should be subordinate to their husbands. All of this is well known. The point has been made: patriarchal religion supports and perpetuates patriarchy.

There are other axioms in my present thinking that are fundamental. For example, I think it is certain that the bonding phenomenon among women, generally referred to as "sisterhood," has deeply spiritual dimensions, even if those experiencing it would not always be inclined to use religious jargon to describe the experience. This spiritual quality of the women's revolution is grounded in our confrontation with nonbeing. As the ultimate aliens, perennial outsiders in a "man's world," women are beginning to be able to allow ourselves and each other to experience nothingness—to see that the entire social structure, meaning structure, and language structure bequeathed to us essentially exclude us as full human beings. This places us consciously in a marginal situation. We become recognizable to ourselves as extra-environmentals. This seeing requires existential courage, and women in our time are in a special way called to be the bearers of this courage, which expresses itself in sisterhood.

Sisterhood, I maintain, is both revolutionary and revelatory. By refusing, together, to be objects—to accept the role of "the Other" —women are beginning to break down the credibility of sex-role stereotyping and bring about a genuine psychic revolution in the direction of what I have called "the sisterhood of man"—that is, in the direction of an androgynous society. By the same token, sisterhod is revelation. The breakdown of the idols of patriarchal religion is happening in women's new consciousness. Out of our courage to be in the absence of these idols—in the face of the experience of nonbeing—can emerge a new sense of transcendence—that is, a new and more genuine spiritual consciousness. This means that a transvaluation of values can take place.

Sisterhood, then, is in a very real sense an anti-church. In creating a counterworld to the society endorsed by patriarchal religion, women are at war with sexist religion *as sexist.* This is true whether we concern ourselves directly with religion or not. Women whose consciousness has been raised are spiritual exiles whose sense of transcendence is seeking alternative expressions to those available in institutional religion. At the same time, sisterhood is functioning as cosmic covenant, proclaiming dimensions of truth which organized religion fails to proclaim. It is a space set apart, in which we can be ourselves. It is also a charismatic community, in which women experience prophecy and healing. Finally, it is an *exodus* community based upon the promise in women ourselves.

These, then, are some basic axioms in my approach to the problem of theology after the demise of God the Father. It cannot be stressed too strongly that the system and the entire conceptual apparatus of Christian theology, developed under the conditions of patriarchy, have been the products of males and that in large measure these serve the interests of sexist society. Given these conditions it is not surprising that women who are attempting to challenge the structures, symbols, and values of Christianity are at times not radical and daring enough, stopping at the goal of mere reforming within pre-established social structures and/or semantic structures that reflect the latter. To get beyond this requires a resurrection experience—beginning to hear and to speak new words. This means real cerebral work, but the work ahead is hardly a merely cerebral exercise. It is growing that has to go on—a growing that takes place *on the boundary* of patriarchal institutions and their legitimations.

What Has to Be Done?

It would in a sense be true but also in a sense misleading to describe what is happening among women (in a specific way among women with "theological training," as it is called) as "the creation of a new theology." It would be misleading if this were taken to mean that the basic assumptions of patriarchal religion, most specifically of Christianity, will go unchallenged—as is generally the case in works that attempt to construct "new theologies," even new radical theologies. I would therefore be hesitant to call what I believe has to be done "a theology of women's liberation," which would mean placing it within the category of theology as presently understood, even "radically." Rather, what I am concerned with is the problem of how the women's revolution can transform Western spiritual consciousness, its symbolizations and its values.

On the other hand, it would be true to speak of the work at hand as the creation of a new theology if the word could be torn free of its traditional limiting associations with patriarchal religion. For its burden is to show how the women's revolution, insofar as it is true to its own essential dynamics, is a deeply spiritual revolution pointing beyond the idolatries of sexist religion and society and sparking creative action toward transcendence. It has a dynamic that extends outward from the becoming of women toward universal human becoming. If it is not short-circuited, this fundamental impulse to which the women's movement is giving expression has spiritual and religious meanings. It has to do with the search for ultimate meaning and reality, which some would call God.

It should be recognized that women have been extra-environmentals in society. Not only have we been excluded from decision-making, but also we have had no essential role in the creation of thought. Under the conditions of patriarchy—which are the only conditions within historical memory—the entire symbol system and conceptual apparatus has been developed by men. It does not adequately reflect or take into account the experience of women and in fact functions to falsify our own self-image and experience. Educated women have often resolved the problems raised by this situation by simply not seeing it—that is, by screening out experience and responding only to the questions considered meaningful and licit within the prevailing thought structures. Women who have perceived the reality of sexual oppression, on the other hand, as Simone de Beauvoir sadly notes, usually exhaust themselves in breaking through to discovery of their own humanity, with little energy left for constructing their own interpretation of the universe. Therefore, the various ideological constructs, among them theology, cannot be imagined to reflect a balanced or adequate perspective. What is required of women at this point in history is a radical refusal to limit our perspectives, our questioning, our creativity to any of the preconceived patterns of a male-dominated culture. When the possitive products of the emerging awareness, questioning, and creativity of women express dimensions of the search for ultimate meaning, they can indeed be called theological, but in the sense of theology that demands the death of the God of patriarchal religion.

As I have indicated elsewhere, theology may be oppressive to women in a number of ways. First, it may be overtly and explicitly oppressive, proclaiming women's subordination as God's will. Second, theology is oppressive even in the absence of explicitly oppressive statements, when exclusively masculine symbolism for God, for the notion of divine "incarnation" in human nature, and for the human relationship to God reinforces sexual hierarchy. Third, even when its basic assumptions appear to be incompatible with sexism and when its language is somewhat purified of fixation upon maleness, theology is damaging if it encourages detachment from the reality of the human struggle against oppression in its concrete manifestations. That is, the lack of explicit relevance of intellection to the fact of oppression in its precise forms, such as sexual hierarchy, is itself oppressive. This is the case, for example, when theologians write long treatises on creative hope, political theology, or revolution without any specific acknowledgment of or application to the problem of sexism. Tillich's ontological theology, too, even though it is potentially liberating in a very radical sense, fails to be adequate in this regard. The specific relevance of "power of being" to the fact of sexual oppression is not indicated. Moreover, just as Tillich's discussion of God is "detached," so also is the rest of his systematic theology. His discussion of "estrangement," for example, when he "breaks" the myth of the Fall, fails to take specifically into account the malignant view of the man-woman relationship which the androcentric myth itself inadvertently "reveals" and perpetuates. He simply generalizes and "goes beyond" the problem. Since the residue of this specific content of the myth still deeply affects Western culture in its attitudes, customs, and laws (e.g., concerning prostitution and abortion), I would suggest that this approach is not adequate.

The Problem of Method

The question arises, therefore, of the method that I propose for dealing with questions of religious symbols and concepts and with ethical problems. I will begin my description of this with some indications of what my method is *not*. First of all, it obviously is not that of a "kerygmatic theology," which supposes some unique and changeless revelation peculiar to Christianity.[2] Neither is my approach that of a disinterested observer who claims to have an "objective" knowledge "about" reality.[3] Nor is it an attempt to correlate with the existing cultural situation "eternal truths" which are presumed to have been captured as adequately as possible in a fixed and limited set of symbols. Such a correlation processs would not be adequate even if understood as *relativizing* of the Christian symbols—that is, even if it included recognition that these symbols need not be seen in a fundamentalist or literalist way.[4] None of these approaches is adequate to express the revolutionary potential of women's liberation for changing religious consciousness and for challenging the forms in which this consciousness incarnates itself.

The method that is required is a method not of correlation but of *liberation*. Even the term "method" must be reinterpreted and, in fact, wrenched out of its usual semantic field, for the emerging theological creativity in women is by no means a merely cerebral process. In order to understand the implications of this process it is necessary to grasp the fundamental fact that women have had the power of *naming* stolen from us. We have not been free to use our own power to name ourselves, the world, or God. The old naming was not the product of dialogue—a fact inadvertently admitted in the Genesis myth in which Adam names the animals and the woman. Women are now realizing that this imposing of words was false because partial. That is, partial and inadequate words have been taken as adequate.

To exist humanly is to name the self, the world, and God.[5] The "method" of the evolving spiritual consciousness of women is nothing less than this beginning to speak humanly—that is, a reclaiming of the right to speak.

It would be a mistake to imagine that the new speech of women can be equated simply with women speaking men's words. What is happening is that women are *hearing* each other and ourselves for the first time, and out of this supportive hearing emerge *new words*.[6] This is not to say necessarily that an entirely new set of words is coming into being full blown in a material sense, i.e., new sounds or combinations of letters on paper. Rather, words which, materially speaking, are identical with the old become new in a semantic context that emerges from qualitatively new experience. The word *exodus*, as applied to the new community of women, exemplifies this phenomenon.[7] The meaning is stripped of the patriarchal context of the biblical writings. So also, the word *sisterhood,* when heard with new ears, no longer means a subordinate semi-brotherhood, but an authentic bonding of women on a wide scale for the first time in recorded history.

Moreover, this liberation of language from its old semantic context implies a breakthrough into new semantic fields. The new context has its source and its verification in the rising consciousness women have of ourselves and of our situation. Since this consciousness contradicts the established sense of reality which is reflected in the prevailing social and linguistic structures, its verbal expressions involve apparent contradictions. This is especially the case since, as I have pointed out, the new words do not constitute a new language in a material sense, but a new set of meanings that clashes with the old. The new words of women's becoming, then, function in such a way that they raise questions and problems and at the same time give clues to the resolution of the problems. When, for example, I write of "the sisterhood of man" there is involved an apparent contradiction and a jarring of images. "Intellectually" everyone "knows" that *man* is a generic term. However, in view of the fact that we live in a world in which full humanity is attributed only to males and in view of the significant fact that *man* also means "male," the term does not come through as truly generic. For this reason many feminists would like to erase the specious generic term *man* from the language. What *sisterhood of man* does, however, is something else. It gives a generic weight to *sisterhood* which the term has never before been called upon to bear. At the same time it emasculates the pseudo-generic *man*. The expression, then, raises the problem of a sexually imbalanced world and it signals other possibilities.

The method of liberation, then, involves a castrating of language and images that reflect and perpetuate the structures of a sexist world. It *castrates* precisely in the sense of cutting away the phallus-centered value system imposed by patriarchy, in its subtle as well as in its more manifest expressions. As aliens in a man's world who are now rising up to name—that is, to create—our own world, women are beginning to recognize that the value system that has been thrust upon us by the various cultural institutions of patriarchy has amounted to a kind of gang rape of minds and bodies.

Feminists are accustomed to enduring such labels as "castrating females." Some have rightly retorted that if "to castrate" essentially means to deprive of power, potency, creativity, ability to communicate, then indeed it is women who have been castrated by a sexist society. However, I would push the analysis a bit further. It is also true that men are castrated by such a social system in which destructive competitiveness treats men who are low on the totem pole (e.g., black males, poor males, noncompetitive males, Third World males, etc.) *like women.* Yet all of these can still look down upon the primordially castrated beings—women. What is happening now is that these primordial eunuchs are rising up to castrate the system that castrates—the great "God-Father" of us all which indulges senselessly and universally in the politics of rape.

The cutting away of this phallus-centered value system in its various incarnations amounts also to a kind of exorcism that essentially must be done by women, who are in a position to experience the demonic destructiveness of the super-phallic society in our own being. The *machismo* ethos that has the human psyche in its grip creates a web of projections, introjections, and self-fulfilling prophecies. It fosters a basic alienation within the psyche—a failure to lay claim to that part of the psyche that is then projected onto the "Other." It is essentially demonic in that it cuts off the power of human becoming.

The method of liberation-castration-exorcism, then, is a becoming process of the "Other" (women) in which we hear and speak our own words. The development of this new hearing faculty and of the new speech involves the dislodging of images that reflect and reinforce the prevailing social arrangements. This happens in one way when women assume active, creative, leadership roles. I am not referring to "role models" in the commonly accepted sense of patriarchy's "models," but rather to the emergence of a kind of contagious freedom—a point which I will develop later.

The dislodging process requires a refusal of the false identity of tokenism. This often implies the necessity for dramatic action, which is many-dimensional in meaning. There is no single prescription for such symbolic acts. They grow organically out of particular situations. They are revelatory, since they not only unmask the fact of sexism but also give signals and clues of future transcendence.[8]

The Unfolding of God

It has been argued that anthropomorphic symbols for "God" are important and even necessary because the fundamental powers of the cosmos otherwise are seen as impersonal. One of the insights characteristic of the "rising woman consciousness" (as Nelle Morton aptly calls it) is that this kind of dichotomizing need not be. That is, it is not necessary to anthropomorphize or to reify transcendence in order to relate to this personality. The dichotomizing-reifying-projecting syndrome has been characteristic of patriarchal consciousness, making "the Other" the repository of the contents of the lost self. Since women are now beginning to recognize in ourselves the victims of such dichotomizing processes, the insight extends to other manifestations of the pathological splitting off of reality into falsely conceived opposites. Why indeed must "God" be a noun? Why not a verb—the most active and dynamic of all? Hasn't the naming of "God" as a noun been an act of murdering that dynamic verb? And isn't the verb infinitely more personal than a mere static noun? The anthropomorphic symbols for God may be intended to convey personality, but they fail to convey that God is "Be-ing." Women now who are experiencing the shock of nonbeing and the surge of self-affirmation against this are inclined to perceive transcendence as the verb in which we participate—live, move, and have our being.

This verb—the Verb of Verbs—is intransitive. It has no object to limit its dynamism. That which it is over against is nonbeing. Women in the process of liberation are enabled to perceive this because our liberation consists in refusing to be "the Other" and asserting instead "I am"—without making another "the Other." Unlike Sartre's "us versus a third" (the closest approximation to love possible in his world), the new sisterhood is saying "us versus nonbeing." When this kind of community-consciousness is present, there are clues and intimations of the God without an over-against—who is Be-ing. The unfolding of the woman consciousness is an intimation of the endless unfolding of God.

New Space: New Time

The unfolding of God, then, is an event in which women participate as we participate in our own revolution. The process involves the creation of new space, in which women are free to become who we are, in which there are real and significant alternatives to the prefabricated identities provided within the enclosed spaces of patriarchal institutions. As opposed to the foreclosed identity allotted to us within those spaces, there is a diffused identity—an open road to discovery of the self and of each other. The new space is located always "on the boundary." Its center is on the boundary of patriarchal institutions, such as churches, universities, national and international politics, families. Its center is the lives of women, whose experience of becoming wrenches the locus of the center for us by putting it on the boundary of all that has been considered central. In universities and seminaries, for example, the phenomenon of Women's Studies is becoming widespread, and, for many women involved, this is the very heart of thought and action. It is perceived as the core of intellectual and personal vitality, often as the only part of the curriculum which is not dead. By contrast, many male administrators and faculty perceive Women's Studies as peripheral, even trivial, perhaps hardly more serious than the ladies' page of the daily newspaper. Most "good" administrators do sense that there is something of vitality there, of course, and therefore tolerate or even encourage Women's Studies—but it remains "on the boundary." So, too, the coming together of women on the boundary of "the church" is for us the center of spiritual community, unrecognized by institutional religion.

The new space, then, has a kind of invisibility to those who have not entered it. It is, therefore, to some degree inviolate. At the same time it communicates power which, paradoxically, is experienced both as power of presence and power of absence. It is not political power understood as the phallic power of patriarchy that objectifies and dehumanizes. Rather, it is a flow of energy which is participation in the power of being. For women who are becoming conscious, this participation is made possible initially by casting off the role of "the Other," which is the disguised nothingness imposed by a sexist world. The burst of anger and creativity made possible in the presence of one's sisters is an experience of becoming whole, of overcoming the division within the self that makes nothingness block the dynamism of being. Instead of settling for being half a person, which is equivalent to a self-destructive nonperson, the emerging woman is casting off the role definitions and moving toward androgynous being. This is not a mere "becoming equal to men in a man's world," which would mean settling for footing within the patriarchal space. It is, rather, something like God speaking forth God's self in women. While life in the new space may be "dangerous" in that it means living without the security offered by the patriarchal system in return for docility to its rules, it offers a deeper security that can absorb the risks that such living demands. This safety is participation in *being*, as opposed to inauthenticity, alienation, nonidentity—in a word, nonbeing.

The power of presence that is experienced by those who have begun to live in the new space radiates outward, attracting others. For those who are fixated upon patriarchal space it is apparently threatening. Indeed, this sense of threat is frequently expressed. For those who are thus threatened, the presence of women to each other is experienced as an absence. Such women are no longer empty receptacles to be used as "the Other," and are no longer internalizing the projections that cut off the flow of being. Men who need such projection screens experience the power of absence of such "objects" and are thrown into the situation of perceiving nothingness. Sometimes the absence of women that elicits this anxiety is in fact physical. For example, when women deliberately stay away from meetings, chapel services, etc., in order to be free to do what is important to ourselves, there is sometimes an inordinate response of protest. Sometimes the absence is simply noncooperation, refusal to play the game of sex roles, refusal to flatter and agree, and so on. This too hints at the presence of another space that women have gone off to and the would-be users are left with no one to use. Sometimes, of course, the absence of women takes the forms of active resistance. Again, it throws those who would assume the role of exploiters back into their sense of nothingness.

In this way, then, women's confrontation with the experience of nothingness invites men to confront it also. Many, of course, respond with hostility. The hostility may be open or, in some cases, partially disguised both from the men who are exercising it and from the women against whom it is directed. When disguised, it often takes seductive forms, such as invitations to "dialogue" under conditions psychologically loaded against the woman, or invitations to a quick and easy "reconciliation" without taking seriously the problems raised. Other men react with disguised hostility in the form of being "the feminist's friend," not in the sense of really hearing women but as paternalistic supervisors, analysts, or "spokesmen" for the movement. Despite the many avenues of nonauthentic response to the threat of women's power of absence, some men do accept the challenge to confront the experience of nothingness that offers itself when "the Other" ceases to be "the Other" and stands back to say "I am." In so doing men can liberate themselves toward wholeness—that is, toward androgynous being. This new participation in the power of being becomes possible for men when women move into the new space.

Entry into the new space whose center is on the boundary of the institutions of patriarchy also involves entry into new time. To be caught up in these institutions is to be living in time past. This is strikingly evident in the liturgies and rituals that legitimate them. By contrast, when women live on the boundary, we are vividly aware of living in time present/future. Participation in the unfolding of God means also this time breakthrough. The center of the new time is on the boundary of patriarchal time. What it is, in fact, is women's *own* time. It *is* whenever we are living out of our own sense of reality, refusing to be possessed, conquered, and alienated by the linear, measured-out, quantitative time of the patriarchal system. Women, insofar as we are becoming who we are, are living in a qualitative, organic time that escapes the measurements of the system. For example, women who sit in institutional committee meetings without surrendering to the purposes and goals set forth by the male-dominated structure are literally working on our own time while perhaps appearing to be working "on company time." The center of our activities is organic, in such a way that events are more significant than clocks. This boundary living is a way of being in and out of the system. It entails a refusal of false clarity. Essentially it is being alive *now,* which, in its deepest dimension, is participation in the unfolding of God.

It should be apparent, then, that for women entrance into our own space and time is another way of expressing integration and transformation. For women, to stay in patriarchal space is to remain in time past. The appearance of change is basically only cyclic movement. Breaking out of the circle requires anger, which enables us to burst out of the alienative circle. Since women are dealing with demonic power relationships—that is, with structured evil—

rage operates as a positive force, making possible a breakthrough. It can trigger movement from the experience of nothingness to participation in being. When this happens, the past is changed—that is, its significance for us is changed. Thus the past is no longer static: it, too, is on the boundary. When women take positive steps to move out of patriarchal space and time there is a surge of new life. I would analyze this as participation in God the Verb that cannot be broken down simply into past, present, and future time, since it is a form-destroying, form-creating, transforming power that makes all things new.

New Being

Elizabeth Cady Stanton, who was probably the boldest thinker of the first generation of feminists, expressed an insight that is important to our present understanding of our situation. She wrote:

> Take the snake, the fruit-tree and the woman from the tableau, and we have no fall, nor frowning Judge, no Inferno, no ever-lasting punishment—hence no need of a Savior. Thus the bottom falls out of the whole Christian theology. Here is the reason why in all the Biblical researches and higher criticisms, the scholars never touch the position of women.[9]

Stanton in this passage has pointed out very accurately the key role of the myth of feminine evil as a foundation for the entire structure of phallic Christian ideology. This myth takes on cosmic proportions when the male's biased viewpoint is metamorphosed into God's viewpoint. With the assurance of this divine disapproval of women, Christianity was able to perpetuate the mechanisms of "blaming the victim" and scapegoat psychology.

Out of the rising woman consciousness is coming a realization that patriarchal religion's treatment of the mystery of evil has been out of focus and therefore that its deepest dimensions have never been really confronted. In dislodging ourselves from the role of "the Other," women are dislodging the problem from this false context. We are thus also moving the question of healing into a new perspective.

The healing process, we are beginning to understand, requires that women cast forth "the Other" within our divided selves, so that the internalized "eternal feminine" image can no longer hold down the authentic self. This process is also in effect an invitation to men to lay claim to their own complete identity. The invitation to wholeness that women are issuing to men has nothing to do with easy reconciliation or cheap grace. Rather, it takes the form of a positive refusal of co-optation.

Since the mystery of evil has been dislocated in patriarchal religious consciousness, it is logical to ask whether the Christian "solution" suffers from a comparable and consequent dislocation. I have already suggested that the idea of a divine incarnation in a male savior may be seen as one more legitimation of male superiority. Indeed, I think that it can be seen now as a perpetuation of the "original sin" rather than as salvation. To put it rather bluntly, I propose that Christianity itself should be castrated by cutting away the products of supermale arrogance: the myths of sin and salvation that are simply two diverse symptoms of the same disease.

I further suggest that when Paul Tillich conceived of the Christ as the New Being he was enunciating a partial truth which has to be dislodged from its context. As in the case of his treatment of the myth of the Fall, he abstracts from the specific content of the symbol—which specific content in fact functions to justify societal structures that oppress us. It is indeed true that our psyches cry out for New Being. However, under the conditions of patriarchy it is most improbable, I think, that a male symbol can function adequately as the bearer of New Being. Inevitably it lends itself to some degree to reinforcement of the structures that oppress, even though, of course, there is an ambivalence about this.

I think, rather, that the bearers of New Being have to be those who live precariously on the boundary of patriarchal space—the primordial aliens: women. The story of Adam and Eve has been described as the hoax of the millennia. So also now the idea of the God-Man (God-Male, on the imaginative level)—the dogma of the hypostatic union—is beginning to be perceived by some women as a kind of cosmic joke. Under the conditions of patriarchy, the role of liberating the human race from the original sin of sexism would seem to be precisely the role that a male symbol *cannot* perform. I am suggesting that the idea of salvation uniquely by a male savior perpetuates the problem of patriarchal oppression.

I see two problems connected with this. First, the symbol itself is one-sided, so far as sexual identity is concerned, and it is precisely on the wrong side, functioning to glorify maleness. Those who would argue that the Christ symbol "can be used" oppressively but need not be used that way should ponder the message that the unique maleness of the symbol itself conveys. When one has grasped this problem, it is natural to speculate that the doctrine of the Second Coming might be a way to salvage tradition—whether this be conceived as appearing in the form of a woman or a group of women or in terms of the so-called feminine characteristics. However, this presupposes that a First Coming actually has occurred. Before moving into the use of this kind of language, then, it would be important to be well aware of what we are about—which brings us to the second problem I have with the traditional doctrine of the "Incarnation"; namely, that a symbol has functioned as model for human perfection. We have come to recognize that it is not adequate for us to accept the manner in which personal symbol-model figures have functioned in patriarchal religion and attempt to change the "content." This takes us, then, to the question of models.

Jesus Was a Feminist, but So What?

In an admirable and scholarly article Leonard Swidler marshals historical evidence to show convincingly that Jesus was a feminist.[10] What I think I perceive happening in the rising woman consciousness is an affirmation that goes something like this: "Fine. Wonderful. But even if he wasn't, *I am.*" Professor Swidler's work has the advantages of striving for historical accuracy and of seeking to maintain continuity with tradition. At the same time, I would have some serious difficulties with him on at least two scores: First, there are difficulties involved in his thesis that one can extract "religious truth" from "time-conditioned categories." Implicit in this seems to be the idea that we can shuck off the debris of past oppressiveness and get back to the pristine purity of the original revelation. The core of my difficulty with this, I think, is that it seems backward-looking, assuming at least implicitly that we should give priority to the past over present experience. My second difficulty is interrelated with this; namely, that there seems to be in this approach an assumption that there *are* adequate models in the past. The traditional idea of *imitatio Christi* seems to be the not-so-hidden agenda of this method.

In contrast to this, I think women are perceiving that patriarchal religion *is* indeed patriarchal and are choosing to give priority to what we find valid in our own experience without needing to look to the past for legitimization of this. I am suggesting: first, that there are no adequate models in the past to guide us in our present situation. Second, I am proposing that the very idea of model, as commonly understood, is one of those conceptual tools of patriarchy that we need to wrench from its old semantic field. We may use the same term, materially speaking, but what we are in fact about, I think, is breaking models. It seems to have been a part of the patriarchal mindset to imitate slavishly a master or father-figure (witness the apprentice system in universities) with an almost blind devotion and then to reject this figure in order to be oneself. (It is significant, perhaps, that the Latin term *modulus* means a "small measure.") This imitation-rejection syndrome is not what is going on with women now. Rather, there is a contagious freedom in the air. Women who are living in the new space, which is on the boundary of patriarchy, spark existential courage in others to affirm their *own* unique being.

As the idea of "model" is torn free from the male context, women call forth in each other the courage to enter the exodus community. *Exodus*, too, we are beginning to hear with new ears. It means "going away" from the land of our fathers. We are going away because of a promise. The promise is not something handed down by a hypostatized God-Father, but rather something that we recognize—that we *hear*—in ourselves and in each other. It is the unfulfilled potentiality of our *foremothers*, whose largely unrecorded history we are now assuming into our present/future. It is the promise in our sisters whose voices have been stolen from them. It is in our own potentiality that we are finding it. In finding it we are participating in the Verb Who is the most active of all verbs.

NOTES

1. See Mary Daly, *The Church and the Second Sex* (New York: Harper & Row, 1968). See also especially the following articles published by her in 1971–72: "After the Death of God the Father," *Commonweal*, March 12, 1971, pp. 7–11; "The Courage to See," *The Christian Century*, September 22, 1971, pp. 1108–1111; "Abor-

tion and Sexual Caste," *Commonweal*, February 4, 1972, pp. 415–419; "The Spiritual Revolution: Women's Liberation as Theological Re-education," *Andover Newton Quarterly,* March, 1972; "The Women's Movement: An Exodus Community," *Religious Education*, September-October, 1972.

2. Karl Barth is, of course, well known for this approach to theology, which holds as sacred the presuppositions of patriarchy. However, I am using the expression in a broader sense, to apply to modern Christian apologists who are attempting to absorb the anger and insight of women without acknowledging the depth of the problem. An example of this is Robin Scroggs, "Paul: Chauvinist or Liberationist?" *The Christian Century,* March 15, 1972, pp. 307–309. Professor Scroggs is concerned to distinguish Paul's own views from those expressed in the pseudepigraphical writings attributed to him. For women this is too little and too late. The women's critique is not of a few passages, but of a universe of sexist suppositions.
3. Male authors who are now claiming that they can write accurately "about women" give away the level of their comprehension by the use of this expression. The new consciousness of women is not mere "knowledge about," but an emotional-intellectual-volitional rebirth. An example of the products of such male claims is Donald McDonald, "The Liberation of Women," *The Center Magazine,* May-June, 1972.
4. This is Paul Tillich's method. Although I find it less inadequate than the methods of other systematic theologians of this century, it clearly does not offer the radical critique of patriarchal religion that can come only from women, the primordial outsiders.
5. See Paulo Freire, *Pedagogy of the Oppressed* (New York: Herder and Herder, 1970). Freire wrote acutely of the namelessness of the oppressed without acknowledging in this book the proto-typical namelessness of women.
6. Nelle Morton gives a profound and moving analysis of this in her article "The Rising Woman Consciousness in a Male Language Structure," *Andover Newton Quarterly,* March, 1972, pp. 177–190.
7. This is the sense in which "exodus" was applied to the historic walkout from Harvard Memorial Church called for in my sermon of November 14, 1971. See Mary Daly, "The Women's Movement: An Exodus Community," *Religious Education,* September, 1972. This article contains the sermon and reflections upon the event by some women who participated.
8. See "The Women's Movement: An Exodus Community," *Ibid.* The Harvard Exodus and its continuing aftermath exemplifies this pro-

cess, involving refusal of tokenism, breaking with the past, dramatic action, and movement toward the really new.

9. Elizabeth Cady Stanton, Letter to the Editor, *The Critic* (1896), cited in *Up from the Pedestal*, edited by Aileen S. Kraditor (Chicago: Quadrangle Books, 1968), p. 119.
10. See Leonard Swidler, "Jesus Was a Feminist," *Catholic World*, January, 1971, pp. 177–183.

VIEW FROM THE BACK OF THE SYNAGOGUE:

Women in Judaism

Gail B. Shulman

"I do not know which is a greater insult to my Creation: to be forever a Daughter of Eve whom men fear through their sin-obssession; or to be forever pedestaled, protected from the storms and stresses and creativities and responsibilities of human development which produces persons and adults. . . . *What do I do with a god who doesn't seem to understand or value my being or becoming, my creation and my creativity?"* [1]

Judaism is a patriarchal religion. One cannot read the Book of Genesis with its numerous references to the God of Abraham, the God of Isaac, and the God of Jacob without realizing the tremendous importance of these patriarchs. And one cannot help wondering (especially if one is female) why there are no references to the God of Sarah, Rebecca, Leah, and Rachel. For a female child, growing up in the Judaic tradition can be a disturbing experience. The model set before her of the traditional Jewish woman is a male-defined, biologically-derived model—that of wife, mother, homemaker, member of the Ladies' Auxiliary, and basically non-participating observer in the rituals and services of the synagogue. It seems a contradiction that Judaism, a religion traditionally concerned with humane and just treatment of oppressed peoples, can be so oppressive to one-half of its own people.

To understand the status of women in Judaism today, it is necessary to investigate both biblical and rabbinic writings while, at the same time, keeping one's historical perspective. Although many

Talmudic* laws grant women the status of a well-loved object or a slightly retarded child, one must remember that, compared to women in other societies *of the time*, who were considered little more than property, Jewish women enjoyed relative freedom. As for the present, the women's movement has come relatively late to Judaism. In comparison with many Protestant denominations which were affected by the first wave of feminism in the nineteenth century, Judaism has remained relatively untouched (for example, the first American woman rabbi was not ordained until 1972). Contemporary Jewish publications have only recently begun to print articles dealing with the status of women in Judaism. Many of the articles are written by men, frequently apologists defending the *status quo* by explaining that in Judaism women are not considered inferior; rather, they are to be praised and glorified . . . when they stay in their proper place. As one contemporary rabbi has commented, "Jewish women aren't oppressed, they're colonized."[2]

Elizabeth Janeway calls this colonization the phenomenon of "Man's World, Woman's Place."[3] In a patriarchal society, the "world" is ordered and defined by men, who then assign women to a particular place. This niche is, of course, the home. In rabbinic writings, the relegation of women to the home is sweetened by the rationalization that her role is of the utmost importance: an "appreciation of the role of women in diffusing and preserving an atmosphere against which the spiritual potential of members of her family might achieve maximum realization."[4] For example:

> Rabbi Jose said: "When a woman keeps chastely *within* the house, she is fit to marry a High Priest and rear sons who shall be High Priests." Rabbi Phinehas bar Hama ha-Kohen says: "This means when she keeps chastely within the house. Just as the altar atones for the house, so does she atone for her house, as it says. 'Thy wife shall be like a fruitful vine within the sides of the house.' [Ps. 128:3—The same word is used for sides here as in the sacrificial regulations with regard to the altar.] "Where shall she be as a fruitful vine? When she is within the sides of thy house. If she act thus, then will thy children be like olives; she will rear sons to be anointed with olive oil of the High Priesthood."[5] (Emphasis mine.)

* Talmud (adj. talmudic)—body of opinions and teachings of laws contained in the Torah. This and following definitions are taken from *Life Is With People* by Mark Zborowski and Elizabeth Herzog, New York, 1971.

This concept of "separate but equal"—male definition of the female as equal so long as her function is separate from his—defines her solely in terms of biology.[6] Paula Hyman best sums up the damage resulting from the idea of separate but equal when she writes:

> Generally it has resulted in the dominant group's defining both the separateness and equality of the second group and justifying that separateness by projecting upon the group being defined a radical otherness. What this has meant in male/female relationships is that the qualities of femininity have been defined by male culture in polar opposition to masculine traits. And uniquely female biological characteristics —in particular, menstruation and child-bearing—have been perceived by men as both frightening and awesome, in no small measure because they are alien to male experience.[7]

And therein lies the problem, for the status of women in Judaism is always that of "other" (inferior or unclean or sinful) and, although she may frequently be placed on a pedestal built of clever rationalizations, she is ever separate, ever in "Woman's Place."

Judaism is dominated by men—the great heroes of the Hebrew Scriptures are male: Abraham, Moses, Joshua, David. The judges and prophets are almost exclusively male: Samson, Jephthah, Isaiah, Jeremiah—the list is endless. The great teachers of the Rabbinic Period too are all men, and today the majority of Jewish scholars are men. The image evoked, of course, is that while these men are fulfilling the *mitzvah** of Torah,† and excelling in their studies, their wives are excelling in their own domain, keeping clean homes, kosher kitchens, and close-knit families.[8] Even Deborah, one of the few actively heroic women of the Old Testament, is belittled in Jewish legend as "subject to the frailties of her sex," since she called Barak to her rather than going to him and extolled herself excessively in her song. The legend continues that as a result, her powers of prophecy disappeared for a time.[9]

Other women who could be considered matriarchs and heroines are criticized too. Sometimes it seems that, as hard as God tried,

* Mitzvah (pl. *mitzvoth*)—divine commandment, good deed, merit.

† Torah—the teachings, the law, the Old Testament, the entire body of Jewish wisdom; also the scrolls containing the Pentateuch.

he could not create a modest obedient woman. A Midrashic* tale describes God's dilemma in creating woman:

He [God] considered well from what part to create her. Said he, "I will not create her from Adam's head lest she be swell-headed [i.e. frivolous]; nor from the eye, lest she be a coquette; nor from the ear, lest she be an eavesdropper; nor from the mouth, lest she be a gossip; nor from the heart, lest she be prone to jealousy; nor from the hand, lest she be light-fingered; nor from the foot, lest she be a gadabout; but from the modest part of man, for even when he stands naked, that part is covered." And as He created each limb, He ordered her, "Be a modest woman."

But even these careful efforts fail:

"I did not create her from the head, yet she is swelled-headed, as it is written, 'They walk with stretched forth necks' (Isa. 3:16), nor from the eye, yet she is a coquette, '. . . and wanton eyes' *(ibid.),* nor from the ear, yet she is an eavesdropper: 'Now Sarah listened in the tent door' (Gen. 18:10); nor from the heart, yet she is prone to jealousy: 'Rachel envied her sister' (Gen. 30:1); nor from the hand, yet she is light-fingered: 'And Rachel stole the teraphim' (Gen. 31:19); nor from the foot, yet she is a gadabout: 'And Dinah went out, etc.' (Gen. 34:1)."[10]

Even the heroic female figures are belittled!

Not only has Judaism minimized its matriarchs, it has suppressed its goddess figure. For Christianity, the Virgin Mary, as unsatisfactory as she may be, fulfills the role of mother goddess. For the writers of the Old Testament, the incorporation of a goddess element was too close to Asherah and the Canaanite fertility cults to be assimilated into the tradition. Instead of direct incorporation, we find traces of the goddess figure cropping up in popular elements of the religion—in various aspects and attributes of Yahweh, some of which later become independent of Him and take on personalities and physical attributes of their own.

In the Apocrypha, Wisdom (*Hokmah*, a feminine noun in Hebrew) is frequently referred to as God's wife, whom he consulted in the process of creation.[11] The Shekinah, which in post-Biblical times denoted God's "in-dwelling presence," gradually underwent personification, becoming a being independent of God. The Sheki-

* Midrash—Various anthologies and compilations of homilies and Biblical exegeses (A.D. 400–500).

nah later took on physical attributes.[12] During the height of the Kabbalah (a mystical Jewish religious movement of the thirteenth through the nineteenth centuries) when the female aspect of the deity became extremely important, the Shekinah was called the *Matronit* ("Matron")[13] who was a kind of consort of Yahweh. The Torah, "clothed" in a silken cover and adorned with ornaments of precious metal, is often spoken of as "God's beloved whom he made the bride of Moses."[14] The Sabbath, too, is often referred to as a queen and bride who descends to earth every Friday evening to fill homes with peace and love.[15]

Despite all of this female imagery, it is important to remember that this is *suppressed* imagery. Many Jewish women who join in the singing of "Come, O Sabbath Queen" on Friday night were taught in childhood that their primary role in life would be that of wife and mother. With the role models given to Jewish women, it is not surprising that so many of them are content to join the women's auxiliary, prepare food for the receptions following synagogue services, and remark that they are not in need of liberation.

Underlying the separate but equal attitude are several "layers" of attitudes toward women. Most of these are set down in biblical and rabbinic writings, but carry grave implications for modern Jewish women. Since women are "other," they are often treated as inferior—not quite property—but certainly not as adult human beings. This attitude is one level removed from the attitude which regards women as "other" but equal. It proceeds from the biological otherness of woman which causes her to be unclean (because of menstruation and childbirth) and therefore inferior.

Woman as Separate (and Unequal)

One of the best-known Jewish prayers is the male's morning prayer, "Blessed art thou, O Lord our God, King of the Universe who has not made me a woman."[16] The corresponding prayer for a female reads, "Blessed art thou, O Lord our God, King of the Universe who has made me according to Thy will."[17] The first prayer has been explained as man's thanksgiving for a "more active and intense (though not necessarily 'higher') spiritual activity than would have been the case had the accident of birth been otherwise."[18] Indeed, had he been born female, he would not, in all probability, have been allowed much spiritual activity. Rabbinic literature makes no requirement that a female child study Torah; one rabbi considers the very possibility an outrage.[19]

The result of this inequality in education led to the inferior status of women in rabbinic literature. For example:

> ... the glory of the Holy One, blessed be He, is derived from the males. David said, "Lo, sons [children] are a heritage of the Lord; the fruit of the womb is a reward" (Psalm 127:3). "Lo, sons are a heritage of the Lord" refers to the males; and if females come, they are also "a reward."

The editor adds, "Though not 'the heritage of the Lord,' inasmuch as they are not expected to acquire Torah or to perform the *mitzvoth* to the same extent as the males."[20]

This is the point at which apologists writing about women in Judaism usually point out that there are recorded instances of scholarly women (e.g., Beruiah[21]) and heroic women such as Deborah and Miriam, but we must understand that these women were exceptions. The prayers recited for newborn infants sum up rabbinic attitudes about women and Torah: for a male child, one says a prayer for "Torah, marriage, and good works," whereas for a female child, one prays for "*reverence*, marriage, and good works."[22] (Emphasis mine.) Although it is a *mitzvah* for a man to study Torah, no such *mitzvah* exists for a woman. Hers is a vicarious life: "Rab asked R. Hiyya: 'Wherewith do women acquire merit?' 'By sending their children [sons, of course] to learn (Torah) in the Synagogue and their husbands to study in the schools of the Rabbis and by waiting for their husbands until they return from the schools of the Rabbis.' "[23]

Since a woman is so bound to home and children and domestic obligations, she is "freed" from those positive ordinances that depend on time of year.[24] This, coupled with the fact that women are not allowed, or at least not encouraged, to study Torah, led to a nonparticipatory role in synagogue rituals which persists today. Women do not count as members of the *minyan*,* cannot lead services, or read from the Torah. And in many synagogues, women

* Minyan—quorum of ten males required for public religious services. In September 1973 the Rabbinical Assembly of America (Conservative) voted to allow women to be counted as members of the *minyan*, subject to confirmation by the rabbi and congregation of each individual synagogue. The ruling does not apply to Orthodox Judaism.

and men sit in separate quarters, a practice which probably originated in the second Temple.[25] (Other reasons for this separation will be discussed below.) In the *shtetl*† where most women knew little or no Hebrew, a *vorsugern* (woman reader) or *voilkennivdicke* (well-knowing one) read and translated the Hebrew into the vernacular.[26] Despite statements to the effect that exemptions from learning and participation are for the purpose of freeing a woman, it seems obvious that the rabbis did not think the female mind capable of such intellectual activity. Woman is associated with *body*, man with *spirit*: "A woman . . . should . . . be a solid, healthy body, whereas a man should be a strong, transcendent spirit."[27] Therefore she takes care of her family's physical needs while her husband takes care of its spiritual needs. "A most efficient division of labor," comments Hyman. "And one which explains the tendency among East European Jewry to relinquish responsibility for the physical support of the family to wives, while husbands withdraw to the *beit midrash*** to study and acquire spiritual merit for the entire family."[28] In the *shtetl*, the woman frequently bore responsibility for the family's economic support too, managing the financial affairs, buying (as well as selling) in the marketplace, while her husband secluded himself in his ivory tower of study.[29]

The fact that women were not encouraged to study Torah naturally led to the belief that they were inferior in the eyes of God. The Midrash *Genesis Rabbah* records statements by two rabbis on the subject of divine speech: "R. Siman and R. Johanan in the name of R. Eleazar ben R. Simeon said: 'The Holy One, blessed be He, never condescended to hold converse with a woman save with that righteous woman [Sarah] and that was through a particular cause.' "[30]

Legal Rights—Woman as "Semi-Property"

In terms of legal rights, one cannot say that the Hebrew Scriptures or the Talmud treats the Jewish woman as a "mere chattel," but, although she was not completely subject to her father or husband, she certainly was not granted the status of adult human being. This may be due in part to her lack of education, as well

† Shtetl—small town, village (usually East European).
** Beit midrash—"House of Midrash," place of study, the synagogue.

as the fact that in the rabbinic period, the marriage age for a woman was twelve and a half years, as compared with a man, who married in his late teens or early twenties. Thus, the child-bride—immature, several years her husband's junior, and without benefit of his education—was incapable of being his equal. Although this was no fault of hers, but rather a result of her socialization, the rabbis repeatedly classed her with children and slaves in legal formulae, deemed her mind "light" (flighty), and did not permit her to take oaths or give formal testimony.[31] The forms of address used by husband and wife underscore the patriarchal structure of the Jewish family in Talmudic times. Whereas she called him "Rabbi," the term a slave or student used to mean "my master," he called her "my daughter." [32]

The Mishnah* speaks of "acquiring" a bride in a section which also deals with the acquisition of slaves, cattle, and property. The bride is acquired in three ways—by money, writ, or intercourse—and upon her husband's death, she is expected to marry her brother-in-law, especially if she is childless.[33] A female child may be sold as payment for a debt (according to Exod. 21:7) by her father, but not by her mother, since the verse begins, "When a *man* sells his daughter as a slave . . ." [34]

Once married, a woman's property becomes her husband's, as well as "aught found by a wife and the work of her hands." [35] In addition, "during her lifetime, he has the use of her inheritance," [36] although in certain circumstances a wife does have the right to earn money and keep her earnings. In the matter of inheritance, males take precedence over females, and a husband has the right to his wife's property, even though he has vowed not to claim it, for such a vow is contrary to Scripture [37] (Num. 27:11).

Only a man can initiate divorce, which is referred to as "putting his wife away," as though she were an animal with some kind of incurable disease. Upon divorcing his wife, a man must return to her the *ketubah,* the dowry which she brought him at the time of their marriage. Some divorces can proceed without the return of the *ketubah,* as in the case of the woman who breaks Mosaic law by serving her husband untithed food, by having intercourse with him during her menstrual period, by failing to set aside a

* Mishnah—collection of the oral Law which is the basis of the Talmud.

dough offering or by making a vow which she does not keep; or a woman who breaks the law of Jewish custom by going out with her hair loose, by spinning wool in the street, by speaking with any man, or by cursing her husband's parents in his presence.[38] Some rabbis claim a wife's unchastity to be the only grounds for divorce (according to Deut. 24:1: "Because he hath found in her indecency in anything"); however, others emphasize the word *anything* and include indecent cooking and the husband's preference of another woman.[39] About the only grounds on which the wife can seek divorce is her husband's denial of cohabitation.[40] Although the woman can initiate divorce, it is on a personal, informal basis between her and her husband. She may set down the conditions of the *get,* or bill of divorce, but only when it is signed by the husband is the *get* valid.[41] The situation of the *agunah,* the woman whose husband has deserted her and disappeared, is a pitiable one indeed, since in a Jewish court he must initiate divorce proceedings. Regardless of the situation in the civil courts, the Jewish woman who desires to remain within her religious community is still bound by this ancient tradition.

Woman as Unclean

Holiness is an extremely important aspect of Judaism. Before holiness became infused with its moral and ethical connotations, it meant "separate" or "other." Thus, God was holy because God was removed, separate from the impurity of humankind, and those humans who came in contact with God or offered sacrifices to God or touched sacred objects had to be clean. One division of the Mishnah is devoted to *tohoroth,* or cleanness. It contains twelve subdivisions describing who and what is clean as well as the various processes of purification. Though many do not apply today, the extensive and detailed laws of *Niddah* (impurity or separation), the seventh order of Tohoroth, are important and "in full force to the present day." [42] Based on Lev. 15:19–24 [43] Niddah elaborates on the laws governing a menstruating woman and prescribes the conditions of her separation. Raphael Loewe, in his book *The Position of Women in Judaism,* calls this preoccupation with "the menstruant" a "conscious emphasis on, and an attempt at the inculcation in a particularly significant area of human interest, of that self-discipline which must be—in all aspects of life—an integral element in the Jewish ideal of cultivating holiness." [44] This concern for holiness, for "cleanness," may be admirable, but the inclusion of menstruating women as unclean individuals, sandwiched somewhere between lepers and those suffering from fluxes is not admirable; it is harmful and demeaning. It says, in effect, that for a great part of a woman's life, a perfectly normal body function renders her unclean, diseased, taboo.

Men have long been awed and frightened by menstruation. Mary Douglas, in *Purity and Danger,* points out that in primitive societies the body is considered an imperfect container, and the margins of the body are thought to be especially vulnerable. Therefore, that which issues from orifices—spittle, blood, milk, urine, feces, tears—is "marginal stuff of the most obvious kind." [45] In the Talmud, taboos against this "marginal stuff" (body emissions) are directed mainly against women. Woman herself is impure and can render a man impure, as can be seen in Exod. 19:14–15. Before God appeared on Sinai, ". . . Moses went down from the mountain to the people; and they washed their garments. And he said to the people, 'Be ready by the third day; do not go near a woman.' " Whether the reason for the interdiction is that any woman (whether she is menstruating or not) is capable of contaminating a man, or because a woman is capable of arousing a man to the point that he forgets about God, is not made clear here. In any case, it is obvious that "people" refers to men, there are no instructions to women to purify themselves by avoiding contact with men.

By Talmudic times, the laws of Lev. 15:19–24 had been expanded to the tractate Niddah, the only subsection of Tohoroth to contain both Mishnah and Gemara.* It is an extensive tractate, treating in minute detail the various situations involving a menstruating woman. The attention given to various colors of unclean blood, for example, rivals an artist's concern for his palette.[46] Moreover, the taboo is not applicable to all discharges of blood ("all bloodstains wherever they are found are deemed clean . . ."), but rather only to those of menstrual blood (". . . excepting those found in rooms or round about places of uncleanness," e.g., chambers used by menstruants).[47] That the uterus itself is considered

* Gemara—the commentary on the Mishnah which along with the Mishnah makes up the Talmud.

unclean is illustrated by a passage from the Mishnah: "All women convey uncleanness (by reason of blood) in the antechamber [vagina] for it is written, 'And her issue in her flesh be blood' " (Lev. 15:19). The Gemara explains that this applies even though the discharge did not flow out of her body while "he that has a flux and he that suffers a pollution do not convey uncleanness unless their uncleanness come forth." [48]

The uncleanness of the menstruant can be transmitted to other persons, especially men, and also to any foods or utensils she may handle.[49] Like a spiritual Typhoid Mary, she contaminates all she touches, and this impurity continues for seven days after the conclusion of the menstrual period, during which time her husband is forbidden, on penalty of a sin offering, to have intercourse with her. After this period of time, the woman undergoes ritual immersion in a "permanently flowing source of water" and is no longer considered unclean. (It is interesting that the end of this period of abstinence coincides with the time of ovulation when intercourse would be most likely to result in conception.) The reasons given for this period of abstinence include those of sexual hygiene, physical health, marital continence (abstinence makes the heart grow fonder?), respect for womanhood, consecration of married life and family happiness.[50] Despite these reasons, many of which seem like farfetched rationalizations, the laws appear to arise from a periodic fear of, rather than respect for, women. Because the laws were written by men, few or none of them restrict men; all of their fears are externalized and projected onto women. Vivian Gornick describes the status of an Orthodox Jewish woman:

> An Orthodox Jewish man may have no physical contact with his wife when she menstruates. An Orthodox Jew may not look upon the face or form of a woman—ever—and he daily thanks God that he has not been born a woman. These strictures are not a thing of some barbaric past, they are a living part of the detail of many contemporary lives.[51]

That such laws contribute to a woman's feelings of negative self-esteem and revulsion for her own body is undeniable. Gornick goes on to imagine the thoughts of a woman in the study of an Orthodox rabbi:

> Why, in this room I am a pariah, a Yahoo. If the rabbi should but look

upon my face, vile hot desire would enter his being and endanger the salvation of his sacred soul; when my body discharges its monthly portion of blood and waste, he dare not even pass over to me an object that will touch my hand, much less sleep with me if I am his wife, for that monthly waste in me is disgusting, and it makes me disgusting. It is offal, dung, filth. It reminds him of what no holy man ever wishes to be reminded; that he is matter as well as spirit. So he has made a bargain with God and constructed a religion in which *I* am all matter and *he* is all spirit; I am . . . the human sacrifice offered up for his salvation . . . so that the strength of concentrated spirituality will course through his veins. . . . Oh, rabbi, . . . if there is no salvation for me there is certainly none for you . . . the bargain you struck is false, . . . your religion is a measure of your fear, not of your courage . . .[52]

In addition, laws governing postpartum uncleanness are equally negative. For seven days after the birth of a male child, a woman is considered unclean; the time is doubled when the child is female.[53] In relation to "hallowed things" (offerings, etc.) a woman after childbirth is "as one that has had contact with one that suffered corpse uncleanness" [54] (*i.e.*, has touched a corpse). During this time, she is also forbidden to visit a sanctuary.[55]

M. Esther Harding, in *Woman's Mysteries,* theorizes that the menstrual taboo was probably the first ever imposed by men and the prototype of all taboos (hence the universal taboo mark is a splotch of red paint).[56] But Harding traces the origin of the aversion to fear of power loss rather than revulsion at uncleanness. Since, in primitive societies, a woman is regarded as possessed by an evil spirit when she menstruates, her power to attract men is increased supernaturally. The primary reaction of a man at this time is not aversion, but intense desire,[57] therefore the rules of taboo surrounding a menstruating woman developed to avert the "chaotic results" of giving in to this irresistible desire.[58] (". . . at her period, the woman's presence would unman men, would destroy the virtue of the war bundle and make arrows glance aside and render spears harmless against the enemy. Put into less concretized form, this means that primitive man under the temptation of aroused desire, could not hold his intention to hunt or fight." [59])

The menstrual taboo is one of the few taboos which do not protect the tabooed individual, but only protect others from her influence.[60] Although Harding's theory that separation of menstruating women ensures the maintenance of order, many psychologists assert that the taboos have grown up as a result of male castration anxiety. Menstrual blood is seen as symbolic of some supernatural wound, an association which arouses man's latent fear of castration.[61] Thus, the taboos are related to sex anxiety and rationalized as concern for cleanness.[62]

Woman as Evil

We have come a long way from woman as the glory of the home to woman as untouchable, but there is yet another deeper "layer"—an attitude that underlies all the others. Most deeply buried in the biblical and rabbinical writers' subconscious is the belief that women are evil and a threat to male well-being. It is a theme older than the Old Testament (Ishtar, for example, is the Babylonian goddess who destroys her lovers). Mary Douglas calls it the " 'Delilah complex,' the belief that women weaken or betray." [63] Despite all the professed concern and respect for women, measures designed to "protect" or benefit the female (such as the no-intercourse-during-menstruation regulation) are usually found to be veiled protection of the male from a corrupting influence.[64]

For Judaism, as well as Christianity, the biblical prototype of the evil woman is Eve, and the story of her creation, subsequent sin, and seduction/corruption of Adam is frequently cited as the basis for male superiority. Rather than blaming the man for his weakness in yielding to temptation, the woman is branded a dangerous, irresistible temptress. The Adam and Eve creation account is a masterpiece of masculine manipulation, beginning with the creation of Eve. Gen. 2:22–25 tells of Eve's creation from the rib of Adam, the first inversion of fact—man is born from woman's body not woman from man.[65] The very removal of the rib carries "symbolic overtones of castration."[66]

The story of Eve and Adam is full of sexual imagery. The snake is a phallic symbol, but is also associated with Eve—the Hebrew word *Havvah* (Eve) is probably related to the Semitic root meaning "snake," a reference to the great Babylonian serpent-mother figure, Ishtar.[67] Among the folklore of many peoples, including the Jews, menstruation is said to be caused by the bite of a snake.[68] A legend from the Midrash *Genesis Rabbah* explains that menstruation is really one of woman's punishments for Eve's sin:

Why does a man go out bareheaded while a woman goes out with her head covered? She is like one who has done wrong and is ashamed of people; therefore she goes out with her head covered. Why do they [the women] walk in front of the corpse at a funeral? Because they brought death into the world, they therefore walk in front of the corpse. And why was the precept of menstruation given to her? Because she shed the blood of Adam by causing death, therefore was the precept of menstruation given to her. And why was the precept of "dough" given to her? Because she corrupted Adam, who was the dough of the world, therefore was the precept of dough given to her. And why was the precept of Sabbath lights given to her? Because she extinguished the soul of Adam, therefore was the precept of Sabbath lights given to her.[69]

The apologist editor notes here: "The attitude toward women is shown in these replies. In accordance with Scripture, she is charged with having brought death into the world through her disobedience, yet her punishment is not to be accursed, but on the contrary, hers is the privilege to emphasize the inviolate character of women to sanctify the bread one eats and spread the cheer of Sabbath, symbolized by light." [70] Alas, the editor can rationalize only the last two precepts as not accursed—the others can hardly be said to "emphasize the inviolate character of women!"

Another Midrashic exegesis cannot be rationalized away. It illustrates the fear of women objectified:

Were it not for the fact that it is written "her hands are as bands" [derived from Gen. 3:16: ". . . Yet your desire shall be for your husband and he shall rule over you."] she would take hold of a man in the street and say to him, "Come and be intimate with me." She may be likened to a biting bitch which its owner holds by a chain, and although it is tied up, it seizes a man by his garments in the street. Similarly were it not for the fact that it is written, "Her hands are bound," a woman would snatch at a man in the street.[71]

This is a description of a "bad [promiscuous] woman." Man is not asked to assume the responsibility to control his desire—rather woman is seen as a subhuman almost demonic creature possessed by uncontrollable desire. Confinement is the only way to control woman. All pretext of glorification has been abandoned, exposing the underlying attitudes—fear and hate.[72]

Lest there be any question about the attitude of the rabbis toward women who had thoughts of equality, the legend of Lilith clarifies all ambiguities. Lilith was originally a Sumerian demon, a child killer whom the Israelites encountered in legends during the Babylonian Exile and incorporated into Jewish folklore. In Talmudic times, Lilith was written into the Creation account as the "first Eve." Lilith was created out of the same dust as Adam, and when he demanded that she obey him, Lilith refused, pointing out that they had been created equal, out of the same material. She then spoke God's name and flew away to the Red Sea, where three angels sent by Adam found her. They ordered her to return, but she preferred to endure punishment and live as a child-killing demon than return to her domineering husband. Throughout Jewish history Lilith has been associated with evil, producing demon-children, menacing newborn babies and dwelling with Satan.[73]

The Talmud is quite explicit in its statements about women and temptation. For example, one man may not be left alone with two women, for the danger of temptation is great; however, one woman may be left alone with two men.[74] The danger of seduction and corruption causes more concern than the danger of rape of the woman, an inversion of priorities which reveals the obvious bias of the all-male authors.

Similarly, another bias is apparent in the case of adultery—a married woman is guilty of adultery when she has intercourse with a man, whereas a married man is guilty of adultery when he has intercourse with a *married* woman.[75] Following the old double standard, a woman accused of adultery must undergo a tortuous and humiliating trial by water, while the adulterer is presumed to suffer the same punishment vicariously—no such ritual is prescribed for men.[76] The message is clear—the married woman is considered private property belonging to her husband and her infidelity is an offense against him. The man, married or single, is master and owner; he commits adultery only when his partner is a married woman and his offense is against her husband, not against his own wife.

In addition, Jewish women traditionally have taken precautions to minimize their powers of attraction. In the *shtetl* (and in some contemporary orthodox communities):

. . . the bride's hair is cut off and for the rest of her life she wears a wig or *sheytl* in order to reduce her dangerous charms. A woman is not supposed to wear short sleeves, and in any case, a man should not study in a room where a woman's arms are exposed. He should not listen to a woman singing, lest it arouse his desire . . .[77]

It is obvious that the idea of separate quarters for women in the synagogue arose not as a result of women's inability to participate in the service, but to put away these distractions, these impure but nonetheless tempting beings, The nonparticipation of women was the result, and not the cause, of their segregation.

Women internalized this destructive image. *Life Is With People,* a book describing life in the *shtetl,* includes several examples of women's self-deprecating comments,[78] as does the Talmud:

R. Johanan relates one day he observed a young girl fall on her face and pray, "Lord of the Universe, Thou hast created Paradise, Thou hast created Hell, Thou hast created the wicked, Thou hast created the righteous; may it be thy will that I may not serve as a stumbling block to them." [79]

There are also many miscellaneous, half-amused, half-derogatory comments about women in the Talmud: "Our rabbis taught: He whose business is with women has a bad character, e.g. goldsmiths, carders, cleaners, pedlars, wool dressers, etc.—of those neither a king nor a high priest may be appointed. What is the reason? Not because they are unfit, but because their profession is mean." [80] . . . "Women are gluttonous; for a woman is suspected of uncovering her neighbor's cooking pot to see what she's cooking." [81] . . . "He that talks much with womankind brings evil upon himself." [82] . . . "Women are said to produce four traits: they are greedy, eavesdroppers, slothful and envious . . . . She is also a scratcher and talkative . . . . She is also prone to steal and gadabout." [83]

The Ancient Laws and the Modern Jewish Woman

Most distressing is the power these laws exert over the modern Jewish woman. The laws are *man*-made, by an all-male establishment, whose sexist exclusivity persists today. Dr. Trude Weiss-Rosmarin points out the discrimination against women in most modern Jewish organizations (as of 1972), including the repression of women professionals in most Jewish educational and all Jewish communal agencies, no women on the boards of many Jewish pedagogic journals, few women educational directors or principals of congregational religious schools, no women on the National Jewish Welfare Boards, only three women listed as administrators of B'nai B'rith Hillel Foundations, and very few women administrators, even in reform synagogues.[84] Few women students are admitted to Jewish seminaries; fewer still are ordained.[85] In most synagogues, women are not called for *aliyoth,** nor can they be counted as members of the *minyan.*[86] A study done by Dr. Bernard Lazowitz at Brandeis University concluded: "Women are becoming the most active members of the Jewish Community, but the Jewish Community is not changing rapidly enough to give official recognition to this new role of Jewish women," [87] but his findings have fallen on deaf ears for the most part. Despite Judaism's ability to apply and adapt the Law to new situations, Dr. Weiss-Rosmarin expresses doubt that *halachic*† laws will be readily changed.[88] It is difficult to change a tradition which has persisted for so long, especially when the changes would be perceived as a loss of power by the dominant group.

Thus the Jewish woman is encouraged by ancient teachings and modern attitudes to devote her attention and energy to the family and other traditionally "feminine" pastimes[89]—Hadassah,** fund-raising, etc. And when she exercises her normal, human aggressiveness and ambition in the only spheres in which she is allowed, she is branded a "Jewish mother," a domineering, neurotic Sophie Portnoy who destroys rather than strengthens her family.

Dr. Pauline Bart, in a fascinating study of depression in middle-aged women, compared middle-aged women who had suffered "maternal role loss" and discovered that of the ethnic groups

* *Aliyah* (pl. *aliyoth*)—literally "going up." Used in reference to the Torah reading. A male member of the congregation is often asked to go up and read from the Torah during the service.

† *Halacha* (adj. halachic)—legal part of the Talmud.

** Hadassah—the Women's Zionist Organization of America.

tested, Jewish mothers had the highest rate of depression, although in non-Jewish families with similar mother/child relationships, the rate of depression was comparable to that of Jewish mothers. She concludes: "Since in the traditional Jewish family, the most important tie is between the mother and children and the mother identifies very closely with her children, the higher rate of depressions among Jewish women in middle age when their children leave is not surprising." [90]

The danger of a mother living for and through her children is obvious. When they leave home, her vicarious life is over and the future seems bleak and empty. The consequences of such a life are detrimental to the Jewish mother as well as her children. And yet, for a traditional Jewish woman, the vicarious life is all but prescribed for her, and the Talmud has no tractates titled "How to Cope Once the Kids Are Grown!"

Throughout many of the sources on women and Judaism runs the motif of Judaism's positive regard for women. And, in their own time, some of the biblical and rabbinic attitudes toward women *were progressive*. But somehow, somewhere, in regard to the status of women Judaism has ceased to progress. Fear lest the sanctity of the nuclear family be jeopardized and old taboos about the sinful, impure nature of women are at the root of the repressive attitude toward women's rights in Judaism. Rabbi Roland Gittelsohn admits:

> Judaism never pretended to extend complete equality to its women. But it consistently expressed far more understanding and acceptance of them as persons than did other civilizations of the time. And properly, fairly understood, it contains an openness to the rights and needs of women which bodes well for tomorrow.[91]

The Talmudic laws came about through a desire to keep Judaism a living, flexible tradition, applicable to a variety of situations. It is pointless for apologists to defend the Talmud as a source of women's rights, and list token women that have "made it," and declare the importance of the stereotypical "feminine" sex role. The solution for Jewish women is not to join the Temple Sisterhood and wait patiently, but to join together *in* sisterhood to confront and change sexist traditions and institutions within Judaism.

Only then will it be possible for a woman to be a Jew *and* a whole person.

NOTES

1. Rev. Peggy Way, "You Are Not My God; Jehovah." Sermon given at Rockefeller Memorial Chapel, University of Chicago, March, 1970.
2. Deborah Weissman, "Toward a Feminist Critique of Judaism," *Congress Bi-Weekly* XXXIX, No. 13 (24 November 1972), p. 14.
3. Elizabeth Janeway, *Man's World, Woman's Place: A Study in Social Mythology* (New York: Dell Publishing Co., Inc., 1972), p. 7.
4. Raphael Loewe, *The Position of Women in Judaism* (London: S.P.C.K. in conjunction with Hillel Foundation, 1966), p. 30.
5. *A Rabbinic Anthology,* ed. C. G. Montefiore and H. Loewe (Philadelphia: Jewish Publication Society of America, 1960), pp. 508-9.
6. E.g., Rabbi David Miller, "Women's Liberation: The Jewish View," *The Synagogue Light* XXXIX, No. 3 (November 1972): "7. They did not grant them [women] 'equality' for which modern women strive, because equality would not apply in that case; women were not equal to men, and men are not equal to women. There is no superior sex. Each is superior *in its own sphere*. Jewish men have seen in women high powers that men do not possess and, in accordance with psychological science, have left to women such duties as they are best adapted to by Nature, in order to accomplish the most efficient results." (Emphasis mine.)
7. Paula E. Hyman, "The Other Half: Women in the Jewish Tradition," *Conservative Judaism* XXVI, No. 4 (Summer, 1972), p. 18.
8. E.g., Mark Zborowski and Elizabeth Herzog, *Life Is With People* (New York: Schocken Paperback, 1971), p. 130. "In her own right, the ideal woman is a good wife and mother and the 'womanish *mitzvoth*'—the three that are special to her—concern her own area, the home. In order to be a good Jew, no matter what else she does or does not do, she must 'take hallah' [bread], light the Sabbath candles, and purify herself in the ritual bath after menstruation."
9. Louis Ginzberg, *Legends of the Jews* (New York: Simon & Schuster, 1961), p. 250.
10. *Midrash Rabbah,* tr. Rabbi Dr. H. Freedman, Vol. I (Genesis) (London: Soncino Press, 1939), pp. 141–142. Dinah was Jacob's only daughter.
11. Raphael Patai, *The Hebrew Goddess* (New York: Ktav Publishing House, Inc., 1967), p. 139.

12. *Ibid.*, p. 154.
13. *Ibid.*, p. 161.
14. *Ibid.*, p. 270.
15. *Ibid.*, p. 27.
16. *Daily Prayers,* tr. A. Th. Philips (New York: Hebrew Publishing Company), p. 21.
17. *Ibid.*
18. Loewe, p. 43.
19. Loewe, p. 29, quoting Rabbi Eliezer, "Whosoever teaches his daughter Torah is in effect teaching her lasciviousness." (*Mishnah,* Sotah, 3:4)
20. *Midrash Rabbah,* Vol. V (Numbers I), pp. 81–82.
21. Loewe, p. 29. But see Zvi Kaplan, *Encyclopedia Judaica, s.v.* "Beruyah" Vol. IV: "Beruyah (second century) is famous as the *only woman* in talmudic literature whose views on *halakhic* matters are seriously reckoned with by scholars of her times." (Emphasis mine.)
22. *Ibid.*
23. *Rabbinic Anthology,* p. 511. The Jewish woman's existence is so bound up with that of her husband that even her status in the afterlife depends on him. "The world to come is pictured traditionally as a glorified, eternalized *yeshiva.* The dutiful wife sits at her husband's feet and enjoys eternal bliss through him. . . . That a woman's husband is somehow the cup from which she sips her heavenly reward is . . . agreed." (Zborowski and Herzog, p. 129)
24. *The Mishnah,* ed. Herbert Danby (London: Soncino Press, 1933), Nashim, Kiddushin 1:7.
25. Solomon Schechter, *Studies in Judaism* (Philadelphia: Jewish Publication Society of America, 1911), p. 316.
26. *Ibid.*, p. 324.
27. Zborowski and Herzog, p. 138.
28. Hyman, p. 18.
29. Zborowski and Herzog, p. 132.
30. *Midrash Rabbah*, Vol. I (Genesis): 387.
31. Loewe, p. 24.
32. *Ibid.*, p. 22.
33. *The Mishnah,* Nashim, Kiddushin 1:1, p. 321.
34. *Ibid.,* Nashim, Ketuboth 6:1, p. 253.
35. *Ibid.*
36. *Ibid.*
37. *Ibid.,* Nashim, Ketuboth, 9:1, p. 257. (Num. 27:11: "And if his father has no brothers, then you shall give his inheritance to his kinsman that is next to him of his family, and he shall possess it.")

"Num. 27:11 has a superfluous 'and he shall possess it' (fem.) interpreted to mean 'and a man shall inherit from his wife.'"

38. *Ibid.*, Nashim, Ketuboth 7:6, p. 255.
39. *Ibid.*, Nashim, Gittin 9:10, p. 321.
40. Manheim Shapiro, "Women in the Jewish Heritage," *Jewish Digest* XIV, No. 1 (October 1968), p. 58.
41. *The Mishnah*, Nashim, Gittin, 2:5, p. 308.
42. *The Babylonian Talmud*, ed. Rabbi I. Epstein. Intro. to Seder Tohoroth, tr. Rev. Dr. Israel W. Slotki (London: Soncino Press, 1948), p. xx.
43. "When a woman has a discharge of blood which is a regular discharge from her body, she shall be in her impurity for seven days, and whosoever touches her shall be unclean until the evening. And everything upon which she lies during her impurity shall be unclean; everything also upon which she sits shall be unclean. And whoever touches her bed shall wash his clothes, and bathe himself in water, and be unclean until the evening; whether it is the bed or anything upon which she sits, when he touches it he shall be unclean until the evening. And if any man lies with her, and her impurity is on him, he shall be unclean seven days; and every bed on which he lies shall be unclean."
44. Loewe, p. 48.
45. Mary Douglas, *Purity and Danger* (London: Routledge and Kegan Paul, 1966), p. 121.
46. *The Mishnah*, Tohoroth, Niddah, 2:6, p. 747: "Five kinds of blood in a woman are unclean: red and black and bright crocus color, and a color like earthy water and like mixed (water and wine). The school of Shammai say: Also a color like water in which fenugreek has been soaked and a color like the juice that comes out of roast flesh."
47. *Ibid.*, Tohoroth, Niddah 7:4, p. 753.
48. *Ibid.*, Tohoroth, Niddah, 5:1, p. 749.
49. *The Babylonian Talmud*, Niddah, p. 31. "A woman's bed and seat are as unclean as that which touches the body of the menstruant herself; just as the touching of her body causes the uncleanness of a human being ... so does the touching of her bed or seat ... cause the uncleanness of a human being. ... It was taught in agreement with Raba: a woman who observed a bloodstain conveys uncleanness retrospectively to foodstuffs and drinks, beds and seats, as well as any earthen vessel even though it was covered with a tightly fitting lid."
50. *Ibid*, Intro., p. xxii.

51. Vivian Gornick, "Woman as Outsider," in *Woman in Sexist Society: Studies in Power and Powerlessness,* ed. Vivian Gornick and Barbara K. Moran (New York: Basic Books, 1971), p. 77.
52. *Ibid.*, pp. 77–78.
53. Leviticus 12:2–4.
54. *The Mishnah,* Tohoroth, Niddah, 10:6, p. 757.
55. Louis Jacobs, *s.v.* "Woman," in *Encyclopedia Judaica,* Vol. 16 (Jerusalem, 1971).
56. M. Esther Harding, *Woman's Mysteries* (London: Longmans, Green and Co., 1935), p. 43.
57. *Ibid.*, p. 47.
58. *Ibid.*, p. 245.
59. Harding. (Also Karen Horney "The Dread of Women," *International Journal of Psychoanalysis* XIII [London, 1932], p. 350: "To primitive sensibilities the woman becomes doubly sinister in the presence of the bloody manifestations of her womanhood. Contact with her during menstruation is fatal: men lose their strength, the pastures wither away, the fisherman and the huntsman take nothing.")
60. William Newton Stephens, "A Cross Cultural Study of Menstrual Taboos," *Genetic Psychology Monographs* 64 (1961), p. 397.
61. *Ibid.*, p. 402.
62. *Ibid.*, p. 398.
63. Douglas, p. 154.
64. H. R. Hays, *The Dangerous Sex: The Myth of Feminine Evil* (New York: Pocket Books, 1972), p. 43. Quoting Horney: "Everywhere the man strives to rid himself of his dread of women by objectifying it. 'It is not,' he says, 'that I dread her; it is that she herself is malignant, capable of any crime, a beast of prey, a vampire, a witch, insatiable in her desires. She is the very personification of what is sinister.'"
65. Geza Roheim, "The Garden of Eden," *Psychoanalytical Review* XXVII (1940), p. 197. See also Basil Moore, "Towards a Theology of Sexual Politics" (private manuscript of University Christian Movement, South Africa), p. 6. "The creation of the female out of the male is a highly emotionally charged symbol. In the sexless atmosphere of the pre-Fall Eden it expresses the creative reproductive ability of the man alone (or the male in dependence on God). Thus is reinforced the idea that it is the male who is the truly and authentically creative human. It reinforces the myth also that the male is the really creative force in reproduction. (The female is merely a passive receptacle.)"

66. Hays, p. 79.
67. Roheim, p. 194.
68. *Ibid.*, p. 177.
69. *Midrash Rabbah,* Vol. I (Genesis), 139.
70. *Ibid.*
71. *Ibid.*, Vol. 8 (Ecclessiastes), 209.
72. Horney, p. 351. ". . . relief is . . . sought and found in the disparagement of women which men often display ostentatiously in all their attitudes. The attitude of love and adoration signifies: 'There is no need for me to dread a being so wonderful, so beautiful, nay so saintly': that of disparagement implies, 'It would be too ridiculous to dread a creature, who if you take her all around, is such a poor thing.' This last way . . . helps to support his masculine self-respect." (See also note 64 above.)
73. Gershom Scholem, *s.v.* "Lilith," *Encyclopedia Judaica,* Vol. 11, p. 246.
74. *The Mishnah,* Nashim, Kiddushin, 4:12, p. 329.
75. Hyman, pp. 19–20.
76. *The Mishnah,* Nashim, Sotah (suspected adulteress), 1:3, pp. 293–4: "They take her to the Eastern Gate . . . where they give suspected adulteresses to drink of the water of bitterness . . . a priest lays hold on her garments—if they are utterly rent, they are utterly rent—so that he lays bare her bosom. Moreover he loosens her hair. . . ." (1:6) "If she was clothed in white garments, he clothed her in black. If she bore ornaments of gold and chains and nose-rings and finger rings, they were taken from her to shame her. He then brought an Egyptian rope and tied it above her breasts. Any that wished to behold came and beheld, excepting her bondmen and bondwomen, since with them she feels no shame. And all women are allowed to behold, for it is written, 'That all women may be taught not to do after your lewdness.'"
77. Zborowski and Herzog, p. 136.
78. E.g., p. 141: "What am I after all, only a sinful woman?"
79. Schechter, p. 318.
80. *The Babylonian Talmud,* Niddah, p. 424.
81. *The Mishnah,* Tohoroth, Tohoroth, 7:9, p. 727.
82. *Ibid.*, Nezikin, Aboth, 1:5, p. 446.
83. *Midrash Rabbah,* Vol. I (Genesis), p. 383.
84. Trude Weiss-Rosmarin, "Women in the Jewish Community," *Jewish Spectator* XXXIII, No. 2 (February 1972), p. 6.
85. Sally Preisand, first American woman rabbi, was ordained in 1972.
86. *The Babylonian Talmud,* Megillah, p. 140: "Our Rabbis taught:

All are qualified to be among the seven (who read), even a minor and a woman, only the sages said that a woman should not read in the Torah out of respect for the congregation."

87. Ruth F. Brin, "Can a Woman Be a Jew?" *Reconstructionist* XXIV (25 October 1968), p. 12.
88. Weiss-Rosmarin, p. 6.
89. Brin, p. 8: "We say to these girls: 'Study to be a good Jew.' Then we add, 'Of course, you may not be a rabbi, a cantor, a Jewish scholar, a Jewish Community leader, the administrator of a Jewish school or a community agency, and with the exception of a few Reconstructionist synagogues, you may not be counted in the *minyan* or be called to the Torah.' Shrugging our shoulders, we add, 'If you are really serious about this, go marry a rabbi.'"
90. Pauline Bart, "Depression in Middle-aged Women," in Gornick and Moran, pp. 110–11.
91. Rabbi Roland B. Gittelsohn, "Women's Lib and Judaism," *Jewish Affairs* XXVII, No. 5 (May 1972), p. 40.

WOMEN AND MISSIONS:
The Cost of Liberation

Alice L. Hageman

Missions and missionaries are not a very fashionable topic today. Those of us who consider ourselves in mainline and sophisticated branches of Protestantism tend to look on missions as something from a more naïve and perhaps more idealistic past. Or else missions are seen as the activity of fundamentalist, fringe sects. What respectable well-educated church person would talk about "Winning the World for Christ in this Generation" in the 1970s?

Yet this topic is central to any consideration of the history of Protestantism in the United States, especially as it involves women. The story of *women* and missions brings into focus those areas which expose our roots—our heritage as female American Protestants—and gives insights into dilemmas facing us as churchwomen today. In particular, the history of women and missions provides material for considering the opportunities, roles, and status of church-employed women; the vitality of the work of lay churchwomen acting autonomously and as volunteers; and the ties among the religious, economic, and political interests of the United States as they expand. In addition, this history may have implications for the current movement for Women's Liberation with its largely white middle-class composition.

Early Days

During much of the nineteenth and early twentieth centuries missions, especially overseas missions, were a primary vocational option for Protestant women who wanted to "serve Christ and His Cause."[1] In addition, women's missionary societies have been one of the few areas of independent female activity in U. S. Protestantism. In the name of missions women have collected funds, made policy decisions, administered programs, recruited personnel, and managed complex overseas operations. These early women had to overcome many obstacles, not least of which was the opposition and assumed superiority of church*men*—clergy and lay.

One clear statement of the latter's position comes out of the Centenary Conference on Protestant Missions of the World held in London in 1888. This conference met at a time when the number of women's boards of missions was growing; when there were more women missionaries, single and married, than men missionaries; and when women's work in missions had won full recognition. A statement made by the Secretary of the American Baptist Missionary Union at that conference sets clear limits to "women's work"; it is a good summary of the prevailing sentiment then, and for years to come.

> While it must be accepted as the duty of single ladies to be helpful in all departments of the work, it ought to be expected of them that they will carefully abstain from any interference with matters not specially committed to their hands. Women's work in the foreign field must be careful to recognize the headship of man in ordering the affairs of the kingdom of God. We must not allow the major vote of the better sex, nor the ability and efficiency of so many of our female helpers, nor even the exceptional faculty for leadership and organization which some of them have displayed in their work, to discredit the natural and predestined headship of man in Missions, as well as in the Church of God: "Adam was first formed, then Eve," and "the head of the woman is the man." This order of creation has not been changed by Redemption, and we must conform all our plans and policies for the uplifting of the race through the power of the Gospel to this Divine ordinance.[2]

Expansion in the numbers of Protestant missionaries sent overseas, both women and men, has to some extent paralleled the expansion of U.S. economic and political interests.[3] One of the more dramatic examples of the overlap between the "secular" and the "sacred" in the United States came in 1898, when the contemplated annexation of Cuba, Puerto Rico, the Philippines, and Hawaii by the United States received enthusiastic support from religious leaders. A citation from the Congregational magazine *Advance* for May 19, 1898, illustrates the sentiment of that time:

> The churchmen of our land should be prepared to invade Cuba as soon as the army and navy open the way, to invade Cuba in a friendly, loving Christian spirit, with bread in one hand and the Bible in the other, and win the people to Christ by Christ-like service. Here is a new mission field right at our doors which will soon be open. Shall we not enter it?[4]

As a result of the Spanish-American War, Protestant missions received the green light to expand in those four countries; within months of the withdrawal of American troops the first Protestant missionaries arrived to begin their work.

It is important to note that this topic of missions and missionaries, despite the many stereotyped assumptions to the contrary, has contemporary as well as historical relevance. In 1970 there were more North American Protestant missionaries overseas than at any other time in our history.[5] Although much Protestant membership in the Third World is now found in Pentecostal and Adventist churches, where there are also many missionaries, nevertheless, the traditional denominations continue to send personnel abroad. According to a recent study of the growth of churches in Latin America, traditional U.S. denominations had sent nearly half of the North American Protestant missionaries working in Latin America in the late 1960s.[6]

Since at most points in the history of U.S. Protestant missions, women have constituted from one-half to two-thirds of the total missionary force, they have been central in the missionary task of saving souls for Christ and perhaps also of winning friends for America. Missions historian R. Pierce Beaver states that "no other form of American intervention overseas has made a more powerful cultural impact than [the] work for women and children."[7] This was the principal interest of women in missions, and a mixture of elements has contributed to their cultural impact. On the one hand, there have been innumerable instances of kindness and generosity and self-sacrifice, acts of faith and courage and heroism. On the other hand, the results of their activity have been, at least in part, to uphold U.S. standards of morality and achievement, to uproot people psychically from their origins, and in many cases to develop in them dependence on and gratitude to their beneficent patrons. The missionaries may also have helped pave the way for inroads in developing countries by western capitalist "technology" and "modernization," changes which have more often benefited the investors than the recipients of that investment.

It is the intent of this essay to tell briefly a complicated story: the interrelation of Protestant women, North American missions, and U.S. imperialism. It will be difficult in the confines of this essay to highlight all the nuances of the story. Since supporting "hard" data are still rather scarce, we must frequently depend on following up provocative hints and making tentative guesses; consequently, this is a preliminary rather than a definitive statement of the interrelation of these three areas of interest.[8] Nevertheless, the essay sketches a working hypothesis, as well as pointing to directions which might profitably be explored further in the future.

Heroines, Martyrs, Failures, and Successes

The missionary in Protestantism has been seen as the very incarnation of commitment and self-sacrifice; in some churches, becoming a missionary was equivalent in dedication to becoming a nun. I remember going to high-school church conferences and being asked for a commitment on that last, supercharged, candle-lit evening. I always understood that the most I could promise (although I could never quite bring myself to do it) was to become a missionary.

The story of women and missions begins in the second decade of the nineteenth century. It has three component parts: married women, single women, and women's missionary societies. It is the story of people probably very much akin to those found in today's liberal seminaries, those who were considered the progressive, advanced, even radical, elements in the churches during the early and mid-nineteenth century. It is a story at the very core of the life of mainline Protestantism.

When the first U.S. missionaries (male) were sent to Ceylon in 1816, it was assumed they should be married. This expectation was confirmed by subsequent experience. Reflecting in 1860 on fifty years of mission practice, Dr. Rufus Anderson, head of the

Boston-based American Board of Commissioners for Foreign Mission (ABCFM), stated:

The experience of the Board favors the marriage of missionaries, as a general rule, and always when they are going to a barbarous people. Wives are a protection among savages, and men cannot long there make a tolerable home without them. When well selected with respect to health, education, and piety, wives endure "hardness" quite as well as their husbands, and sometimes with more faith and patience.[9]

Although her status was more than that of a pastor's wife, the woman who accompanied her mate to the mission field was for many years designated "assistant missionary"—or subsidiary to her husband, who was the person appointed by the sending agency. Yet from the time of their departure it was assumed that, although the "domestic" sphere was to be the focus of her life, the missionary wife would also develop work with women and girls. As the Reverend Jonathan Allen pointed out in his sermon to two of the first three missionary brides:

It will be your business . . . to teach these women. . . . Go then, and do all in your power, to enlighten their minds, and bring them to the knowledge of the truth. Go, and if possible, raise their character to the dignity of rational beings, and to the rank of Christians in a Christian land. Teach them to realize that they are not an inferior race of creatures; but stand upon a par with men. Teach them that they have immortal souls; and are no longer to burn themselves, in the same fire, with the bodies of their departed husbands. Go, bring them from their cloisters into the assemblies of the saints.[10]

In many instances the missionary wife provided the wedge for her husband's entry into local life. For example, during their first five years in Burma, the pioneer Judsons, Adoniram and Ann, did not make a single male convert. However, it is reported that Ann, the first of Adoniram's three successive wives, met regularly during this same period with a group of twenty to thirty women to talk "about the God who, to their inexpressible astonishment, loved women equally with men."[11]

Climate and conditions of public hygiene in strange lands were often inimical. Women maintained households, bore and raised (and frequently buried) children in conditions far more difficult than at home. Numerous missionaries lost one or more mates during their service abroad. Many a widow remained to continue her ministry alone, or to marry a widower.

It was assumed that no man would go out without a wife, as described in the words of Dr. Rufus Anderson, as "a friend, counsellor, companion, repository of [his] thoughts and feelings, partaker of his joys, sharer in his cares and sorrows, and one who is to lighten his toils, and become his nurse in sickness."[12] It was equally assumed in the early years of missions that no woman would go out in any capacity other than as wife, although some, as noted above, were allowed to remain overseas when widowed.

"Betsey Stockton, colored woman, Domestic Assistant"[13] was the first single woman not a widow sent overseas. Little is known about her except that she went to the Sandwich Islands attached to the family of the Reverend Charles S. Stewart, and that she had been born a slave in Princeton, New Jersey, in 1798. During two years, from 1823–25, she conducted a school which was described as "well-run." She was obliged to return to the United States when Mrs. Stewart's health failed.

Cynthia Farrar was the first *un*-married woman sent overseas specifically as "assistant missionary" by any agency: in 1827, by the American Board, to the Marathi mission in India.

During the following three decades, however, mission boards remained reluctant to employ unmarried women. Those sent had virtually no freedom of residence, for they were required to be attached to the household of a missionary family. There, of course, they ran the risk of becoming assistants to the assistant missionary, consumed with the work of operating that household and prevented from doing the tasks for which they had come. In most cases their wider work was restricted to educational activities for women and girls.

By 1860, year of the semi-centennial of foreign missions, probably not more than fifty single women had been sent overseas, thirty of them by the ABCFM. It was only after that point, with the development of relatively autonomous Women's Boards of Missions, that single women went overseas in significant numbers and with responsibilities greater than those of the wifely "assistant missionary."

Long before that development, however, Protestant women in the United States had been working actively on behalf of missions. The

Boston Female Society for Missionary Purposes, established by Miss Mary Webb on October 9, 1800, was the first formal group organized by women for the support of missions. This society and its many successors developed as groups which raised money and spread information about missionary activities, on the frontier and overseas. By and large they functioned in association with, or as auxiliaries to, the mainstream male-dominated organizations. Constantly they were subjected to criticism and questions; rarely were they allowed any part in deciding how the money they had raised would be spent, nor any opportunity directly to support their area of greatest interest, work with women and girls.

Finally, around the time of the Civil War, Protestant women began to assert their specific interests in missions—although admittedly in the genteel, nonconfrontational manner befitting Christian ladies. In 1861 the nondenominational (or interdenominational) Women's Union Missionary Society was organized, and in 1869 the Boston-based Woman's Board of Missions of the American Board (Congregationalist) was incorporated. The latter third of the nineteenth century was marked by the proliferation of mission societies: in 1860 there were five major and four minor boards; by 1900 there were ninety-four sending and forty-three supporting agencies. The growth of women's boards was especially notable, from none in 1860 to forty-one U.S. and seven Canadian by 1900, or some one-third of the total.[14]

Although the women's societies carried on a variety of activities, Protestant women of the nineteenth century knew—and stayed in—their place. For years these women acquiesced in the prohibitions against their speaking in public, particularly in mixed gatherings. They accepted restrictions on their raising funds at public assemblies, and on developing autonomous activities which might threaten the work of the General Boards. They submitted to the necessity of petitioning the parent denomination for permission to establish any independent or even auxiliary group in which women would have a major say in program, policy, and budget; any such request met with resistance, and frequently with open opposition. Patiently, Protestant women accepted their position of being without voice or vote, dependent on persuasion and good works to make their case. As one Methodist woman noted, after the Woman's Foreign Missionary Society finally won its "independence" in

1888, "We are shown through many perplexities, how to manage that doubtful problem, the reluctant brethren."[15]

Despite the anxieties of churchmen, both clergy and lay, Protestant women interested in missions in the latter half of the nineteenth century did not ally themselves with those others of their time struggling for the rights of women in the United States. They seemed to feel more at ease in social service activities and charitable deeds of mercy than in participating in the more confrontational tactics and disruptive institutional goals of the suffragettes. One Kentucky journalist reported after a meeting of the local women's missionary society, "Two things can be said of this gathering of women; it was not in the interest of woman's rights nor suffrage, nor had they a crank among them."[16]

Once the Women's Boards were established, women had the opportunity to spend the money they raised, to make policy decisions, and to carry out their own administration. Their work generally followed a pattern established by the Congregationalist women: raising funds to support single women missionaries and to pay the expenses of work for women and children; disseminating missionary information and fostering missionary spirit through local branches in the churches; and training children for participation in missions. Their recruitment efforts met with notable success; in six U.S. denominations, female personnel went from 49 per cent of the total number of missionaries in 1830, to 57 per cent in 1880, to 67 per cent in 1929.[17] Women's Boards were also very effective in raising money; in 1910, when the fiftieth year of the women's missionary movement was marked, it was reported to the Interdenominational Conference of Women's Boards of Foreign Missions of the United States and Canada that among the fruits of the year-long Jubilee celebration were "joy, knowledge, faith, prayer, humility, and love expressed in an offering of $1,030,000."[18]

The development of Women's Boards meant that single women who became missionaries could be sent out to assume major responsibilities and to act as independent beings in ways which were virtually impossible for them in their own native land. The story of the work of these women, of their ventures into new (to western whites) territory, of their endurance of innumerable physical hardships, crippling diseases, and early deaths provides one heroic saga after another. The following three persons are especially remarkable and well known; their stories illustrate the kinds of work developed by single-women missionaries.

Isabella Thoburn was the first missionary appointed by the Woman's Foreign Missionary Society of the Methodist Episcopal Church in 1869. Her school in Lucknow, India, expanded from a rented room in a bazaar, to a missionary bungalow, to nine acres for a boarding school which eventually concentrated on high-school-level work, and a series of training schools for Bible women. These indigenous women itinerated among rural villages as Bible teachers and evangelists, and recruited new women converts. In the early twentieth century a woman's college was established in affiliation with Calcutta University, and named for its founder, Isabella Thoburn.[19]

Lottie Moon went to China under Southern Baptist auspices in 1873. With her sister, Edwinia, she operated out of a school in Tengchow, Shantung Province. She felt her real calling was to be an itinerant evangelist in the interior, and so she traveled throughout a large region, taking the Gospel to women and girls in small villages. During the revolution of 1911 famine hit her area; she gave most of her salary for food to feed those around her, and virtually starved in identification with the people of Tengchow. She died on Christmas Eve, 1912. During her lifetime Lottie Moon carried on extensive interpretative correspondence with women in Baptist churches in the United States; her work stimulated the organization of the Women's Missionary Union in 1888. Lottie Moon is stll regarded as the "patron saint" of Southern Baptist missions, and as recently as 1966 the Lottie Moon Christmas offering, whose goal was at $14,500,000, was oversubscribed![20]

Dr. Ida Scudder was born in South India in 1870 of Reformed Church missionary parents. One night three different men came to her parents' house, asking her to assist their wives in childbirth. Since she had no medical training, she said she could not do that work alone, but would gladly help her doctor father. The husbands refused to allow any man to attend their wives, and all three women died. As a result of that experience, Ida Scudder resolved to become a doctor. She established the first women's hospital in Vellore; from this hospital, clinics treating tens of thousands of women developed throughout South India, and finally a women's medical college to train Indian women was begun in Vellore in 1918. It is interesting to note that when missionaries were listed by sex, there were three categories for women: married, unmarried, and doctor. Apparently if a woman had medical training, then she could be identified in terms of her work rather than her marital status![21]

There were great pressures on single women to succeed, to emulate the missionary heroine and furnish the supporting group back home with tales of conversion and institutional growth. Yet not all the single women who went abroad as missionaries offer success stories to history. The strain of life alone among strange people and unfamiliar ways took a heavy toll. Although some women missionaries seem to have been self-sufficient, others needed and sought out personal support, encouragement, and companionship, either in marriage or in close relationship with another woman. Still others denied those needs and gradually became, as a nineteenth-century missionary to China noted, "one-sided or eccentric, or narrow, from living long in isolated places. . . ."[22] Some succumbed to the pressures and either died young or returned home early.

Many single women who left the United States married after their arrival on the "field." The female missionary societies considered such marriage the cause of many "hindrances and discouragements,"[23] and did all they could to prevent them. For, as R. Pierce Beaver has pointed out: "The whole women's missionary movement was built upon a celibate order of life-career missionaries maintained at a subsistence level."[24] If a woman married or resigned before the end of her first term she was required, by a signed pledge, to return her travel and outfit allowance and sometimes even her salary—or to have those costs borne by the Board of her husband-to-be. In several instances young women were virtually accused of being unfaithful both to Christ and to the missionary society if they married!

Some women missionaries did not marry—thereby avoiding the wrath of the women's society—but rather developed relationships with one another which provided companionship and support. The Rankin sisters, Dora and Lochie, Southern Methodists stationed in Nantziang, China, had such devotion for one another. When Dora died, Lochie wrote, "We never paraded our love, but she was intertwined with every fiber of my being."[25] Still, Lochie refused to consider changing either her work or location after Dora's death: "Dora was one half of my life; the work at Nantziang is the other. I cannot leave that."[26]

In other instances, single women developed a close relationship with a woman from the country in which they worked. Liiivati Singh became the close friend and companion of her teacher and mentor, Isabella Thoburn. Miss Singh visited the United States with Miss Thoburn, obtained a graduate degree, and taught for many years at Lal Bagh, the school established by Miss Thoburn. She contributed many invaluable and insightful reminiscences to Miss Thoburn's biography.

In the face of loneliness and isolation, self-denial became the hallmark of many missionary women. Methodist missionary Laura Haygood never felt really at home in China, where she went as a middle-aged woman to work in school administration.

> It is almost impossible to find congenial companionship with the Chinese. . . . We may enter in some measure into their lives, because we make it the business of our lives to do that . . . but, save for that part of our lives which has been given to work for and with them, our lives are closed to them. . . . Can you imagine what it means to live in a Chinese city with not one of your own race near you?[27]

Yet she did not leave China even when dying of cancer. "I have tried to live for duty these many years," was her response to her sister's plea that she return to the United States.[28]

Although countless missionaries suffered from ill health and recurrent bouts with diseases such as cholera, dysentery, and malaria, probably more frequently than the women's societies cared to publish or perhaps even recognized, the illnesses were as much psychic as physical. Many women cracked under the strain, and either returned home or died after a brief period overseas. One early missionary to Liberia was said to have spent her last days "in mental affliction and drug addiction."[29] Dr. Harriet Woolston returned to the United States after only a year in India; she died, "insane," a few years later.[30]

The popular image of the single-woman missionary as Protestant equivalent of the nun may have some truth, although in some ways the life of the missionary was even more difficult. She had made no vow of celibacy, yet faced virtual charges of betrayal if she married. She had not joined an order, and therefore did not have the explicit and intentional support of her sisters. That the women's missionary societies sometimes tried to play that support role is indicated in a letter from Mary Mason, president of the New York

Female Missionary Society, to Ann Wilkins, the missionary the organization supported in Liberia from 1836 to 1857:

> You may always look to our Female Mission Board as to a family of sisters, who are ever ready to sympathize with you in all your afflictions and, as far as in their power, to lighten your burdens and to assist you in your labor of love.[31]

Even when such assurances were offered, however, the mission societies were far away and of little help in meeting the day-to-day physical and emotional demands of life in a foreign country. Indeed, the self-sacrifice required of Protestant single-women missionaries may have demanded even more than that state assumed by Roman Catholic nuns in their vows of poverty, chastity, and obedience.

Although not *all* women missionaries were successful and self-sufficient, the Women's Boards did support several generations of strong, courageous, independent women workers. They also carried through on their concerns for women and girls and developed institutions and programs all over the world. They accumulated extensive resources and made efficient use of them. In fact, their use of resources may have been *too* efficient; the Women's Boards were known for paying meager salaries and for giving very poor retirement benefits.

Although still operating under denominational umbrellas, the Women's Boards developed virtual autonomy from the General Boards (frequently to the displeasure of the men who controlled those boards) and held out for establishing their own priorities. However, during the early twentieth century the General Boards became very anxious to absorb their energies, programs, and especially their funds. The final chapter in the story of women and missions is that of how slowly—denomination by denomination—the Women's Boards disappeared.

The women succumbed to a variety of pressures: appeals to denominational loyalty; criticisms about inefficiency and duplication of effort; assurances that they would be amply represented in decision-making capacities and their concerns would be carried on in the new "integrated" structures. However, the experience of women in several denominations subsequent to "integration" indicates that the seductive promises were rarely translated into reality, at least not after the first few years. Their experience teaches the power of separatism, and the dangers of co-optation.

Most of the "integration" took place during the 1920s. Usually it was preceded by protracted negotiation; in the case of the Presbyterians, it was effected through action of the General Assembly in 1922, without consulting membership or executives of either the Board of Foreign Missions *or* the Woman's Board of Foreign Missions. The Women's Division of the United Methodist church was the last holdout of the mainline denominations. It was finally merged in 1964.

This story of the demise of the Women's Boards is illustrative of the phenomenon which Beverly Harrison terms "soft feminism."[32] Despite their ability to develop and maintain independent activity, women in the churches were unable to withstand attack and unwilling to be confrontational; they were too ladylike to fight back. On the other hand, although the number of U.S. missionaries abroad has more than doubled in this century, the number of single-women missionaries abroad has remained virtually static since 1925. This may mean that, although these women were unable to struggle actively and openly to defend their own interests, they did at least develop a pattern of resistance and non-cooperation.

Missionaries: Agents of Imperialism?

Women missionaries, more numerous than men at least prior to the dissolution of the Women's Boards, deserve attention in any serious consideration of the ties between missionary activity and imperialist expansion.

What are some of those ties, and how do they operate?

Imperialism, as used in this paper, refers to "the economic domination of one region or country over another—specifically, the formal or informal control over local economic resources in a manner advantageous to the metropolitan power, and at the expense of the local economy."[33] In assessing the effects of missions, we are considering the phenomenon of *cultural imperialism,* the *cultural* domination of one region or country over another, that process by which a dominant power influences the changing culture of another country in such a way that the cultural values and norms of the dominant power become internalized as the values of the local area/congregation/mission-school graduate.

Han Suyin has written about the "long-term missionary investment" which Americans made in China.[34] She maintains that, although American business investment was only 6 per cent of total foreign investment in 1930, U.S. influence far outstripped that of either the British or Japanese, whose total assets were far greater. She cites a French diplomat as saying, "Spiritual investment pays greater dividends than any other form," and she goes on to assess the effect of some missionary-operated educational institutions in China. She describes the founding of Yenching University as a Christian rival to the atheistic, left-wing focus of Peking University. Miss Han speculates that Yenching's missionary-educator president, John Leighton Stuart, "felt an educated, American-Christian Chinese elite, self-propelled and self-supporting, would play a role of great benefit. That it would primarily be shaped to preserve America's best interests and markets in China may not have occurred to him." One indication of the interrelation between public and private sectors is that Dr. Stuart was subsequently U.S. Ambassador to China from 1946 to 1949.

An example of the explicit expectation of "pay-off" for spiritual investment comes from Cuba. Warren Candler was Methodist bishop of the Southeastern jurisdiction which then included Cuba, founder of prestigious Candler College in Havana, and brother of Coca-Cola head Asa Candler. Bishop Candler once described the interdependence of religious and commercial activity thus:

> The North American and South American continents cannot be bound together firmly by ties of commerce alone. They will become fast friends when they *think and feel alike*. Our universities, if they are richly endowed and adequately equipped, will serve this end more effectually than all the consuls and commercial agents who have been or can be engaged to accomplish it. In this matter our commercial interest and our religious duty coincide.[35]

Although some may consider that the export of Coca-Cola and Southern Methodism are legitimately linked and probably brought great benefit to the people of Cuba, others may object to the conflict of interest exemplified in the story of the Candler brothers.

The experience of Protestantism in Cuba has shown the effects of training people to *think and feel* like their North American counterparts. When the Cuban Revolutionary government came to power, most of the Cuban Protestant pastors left the country. They saw their interests and identity to lie more with the mission boards which supported them than with their fellow Cubans. There are stories of many a pastor who said, at his arrival in New York or Miami, "Those who stay behind are traitors. I'm loyal to the Presbyterian (or Methodist, or ———) Board of Missions."

The assumption of cultural superiority which has served as rationale for the intervention of overseas missions has sometimes been stated explicitly. One of the clearest such statements, called *The Individual and Community Need in Latin America of Evangelical Principles*, came out of the Panama Congress in 1916. This statement was formulated to justify Protestant mission activity, both male and female, in Latin America, an area whose people had previously been considered "Christian" and therefore not in need of such attention. It summarizes the tenets of the expansionist American civil religion which still so deeply infuses the rationale for much U.S. activity outside our borders.

The peoples of the north of Europe, the British Isles, the United States of America and Canada, as a result of the Reformation, their access to the open Bible, the tendencies toward democracy in church and state, and the interplay between the scientific and ecclesiastical movements have come to have views of the Christian faith and the Christian life which have proved to be truly formative in the individual and social expression of religion. It is confidently believed that these views would be of large value to the peoples of Latin America, and this belief is held without the denial of the presence of much essential truth in the ancestral faith of the Latin Americans. Clearly that faith has had moral and spiritual values of large benefit to those who have received it. But it is confidently believed that in America, the purest streams of thought and life flowed along the northern parallels. We have had the full benefit of the movement in Europe which delivered people from rigid formalism in religious life and from despotism in national life. This inheritance was denied to those republics which found their historic origins in the monarchies of southern Europe. We are persuaded that the truths and principles thus gained should be shared with our neighbors, who are rich in so many gifts and graces. Historically those truths belong to democracy. The brave republics of Latin America, many of which have fought their way to an acknowledgement of popular rights and government, are entitled to a share in those doctrines which everywhere have inspired such rights and have been the guardians of such government.[36]

This was the official statement of representatives of forty-four U.S., one Canadian, three British, and two Jamaican Protestant mission agencies—including some women's societies. No doubt those present genuinely believed that their efforts would bring great blessings to the peoples of Latin America. Yet that conference of 1916 paved the way for the situation today, with one-third of all U.S. missionaries located in ripe-for-revolution Latin American countries. Some of those North Americans who are currently missionaries in Latin American countries are supportive of movements for socioeconomic change on that continent. Many others, however, cooperate more with various U.S. Government and private programs, and with those established powers who seek to reinforce a repressive *status quo*, rather than with those forces which seek liberation from oppressive conditions.

The work carried out by women missionaries was directed primarily to women and girls. It had three foci: evangelization, education, and health. In many instances medical work was the inroad for creating a climate favorable to other types of missionary activity. That work oriented toward ideological formation, "education (or training) for Christian character," has probably had the most impressive demonstrable results, especially on the middle sectors of given societies. As women missionaries did the "woman's work" of staffing schools and hospitals, they quietly communicated through teaching and example their identification with and loyalty to their culture of origin.

Probably it is inevitable that people, including women, will shape their work according to their own experience and background. This does not necessarily mean that there was malice, or even the intent to dominate, in their activity. But in countries with poor educational and health facilities, how can education based on assumptions foreign to the culture in which it is being offered—the kind which Protestant women excelled in providing—help but have a significant impact on shaping the values and loyalties of those being educated and cared for, those who in turn become the educated class?

Whatever the intent, the effect of their activity has been to implant U.S. values, develop dependency on U.S. patrons, and train people in how best to function in a U.S.-type society. It has also contributed to the upward mobility of a select few who have either risen to positions of prominence within their own country or been able to leave for other countries—in which English is often the major language! Frequently those served already came from the upper class of their society. The strategic argument was that if the rulers were converted, the masses would follow.

Many missionaries who went to India concentrated their attentions on women in the *zenanas*; they entered the harems of the upper class to teach Bible and English, instruct the cloistered women in sewing and embroidery, converse and read with them, tell them about life in Europe and the United States, and in general help break the monotony of their existence.

McTyeire, the school established by Mary Haygood in 1892, was to become "the foremost private girls' high school in the Shanghai area."[37] Its student body was composed of girls from wealthy non-Christian families and girls from more modest Christian families. Today, the Methodist-supported Robinson School in San Juan has a reputation as a "finishing school" for upper-middle-class Puerto Rican young women.

Not all missionary attention has been directed to the upper class, however, but that which went to lower-class women has had mixed results. Missionary activity which went beyond an introduction to basic health, sanitation, literacy, and educational training often meant, implicitly or explicitly, training students in Anglo-Saxon language, literature, and mores rather than immersing them in the indigenous civilization. As Miss Singh said about the beloved Isabella Thoburn, "She taught us English literatures, and I can never forget how her enthusiasm for heroes and poets kindled a like enthusiasm in us."[38]

The success of a missionary was sometimes measured, as was that of Mrs. Emma V. Day in her work in the Congo, by clear U.S. cultural norms. It has been said that she was—

> having a woman's and a mother's part in caring for the children at the mission, and so training the girls that, after a few years, the naked children of the bush were transformed and young women were wearing neat dresses of their own making and able to do the duties of a civilized and refined Christian home.[39]

Many lower-class women who were converted were consequently cast out of their families and completely uprooted. The church could offer them only virtual starvation stipends at the very bottom of the ecclesiastical ladder as "Bible women." Thousands of such women, often characterized as devoted, faithful, and energetic, were thus employed in India and China. On the other hand, some missionaries bemoaned the fact that missionary training led more to upward mobility on the socioeconomic ladder than to increased zeal for the spread of the Christian Gospel.

Missionary activity has affected more than the missionaries and the missionized. A substantial part of the story of missions, especially of the women's missionary societies, is the story of developing local, stateside interest and support. From the very beginning women missionaries were heroines to the supporting church members at home, sources of inspiration, and reasons for continued prayer and fund-raising. As Beaver notes, "The missionary wives vicariously represented the women at home, working out in practice their concern for the salvation of mankind and especially their heartfelt burden of responsibility for the liberation of women in Eastern lands and primitive societies."[40] Such heartfelt identification with missionary activity has often functioned to rationalize the total U.S. presence abroad—economic, military, and political, as well as religious.

A major goal in many denominations has been, and continues to be, the establishment of a mission support unit in each congregation. Even today many women exercise leadership on a local level in relation to missions. For example, a survey of church activity conducted by the United Methodist Church in 1971 revealed that 84 per cent of the heads of Commissions on Missions in parishes that year were women.[41] Women in local units such as these have served to raise funds, provide support, and to act as linkages between persons in local congregations and those in the field. One wonders what might have been the effect if their energies had been focused elsewhere. For example, what would have happened if, instead of providing support for missionaries intent on saving souls and performing acts of charity, those women had worked to change those corporate and governmental policies within the United States which helped perpetuate conditions of oppression abroad?

In addition to diverting attention away from the *cause* of oppression to its *effects*, knowledge of the presumed good works of the missionaries may have acted to salve possible uneasy consciences about the effects of other U.S. activity abroad. After all, what if the American military invades or bombs? What if American businessmen exploit the natural resources and labor of poorer countries? We still have our missionaries building schools and hospitals and teaching people about the love of God in Christ Jesus! But does the Christian imperative "Go into all the world . . ." really justify historical ties between the religious and economic expansion of the United States?

Today we reap the harvest sown by our foremothers and forefathers. Missionary operations continue, stronger than ever. The proportion of North Americans among missionaries has grown from one-third at the turn of the century, to some 70 per cent of the world's total in 1970; the expansion of missionary activity has kept pace with the growth of other U.S. interests abroad in the twentieth century. In 1969 there were some 33,290 North American Protestant missionaries serving overseas—almost five times as many missionaries as Peace Corps volunteers (6,900 in 1970).[42] Although the number of single-women missionaries has remained constant since 1925, the number of married women has grown apace; and in many countries the work of the single women sent out in the late nineteenth and early twentieth centuries continues to bear fruit.

It is no surprise, then, that large numbers of missionary personnel can be found today in Brazil, Japan, Mexico, Taiwan, South Korea, and South Africa, where U.S. interests are strongly established, or in India, the Philippines, and Thailand, where they are under attack. It is interesting to note that in the years since the Cuban Revolution of 1959 the proportion of North American Protestants sent as missionaries to Latin America has grown from one-fourth to one-third of the total of North American missionaries in the world.[43]

The Cost of Liberation: A Study in Contradictions

The preceding pages have given some indication of the ties between the expansion of Protestant missions and U.S. economic domination. But how do *women* and missions and imperialism all fit together?

There are three possible interpretations. First, the position of women within the churches parallels the position of colonized peoples, *e.g.*, oppressed and exploited at home and abroad; second, women, although oppressed at home, have acted as agents of similar or equivalent oppression when they went abroad as missionaries; third, there is truth in both positions. The story of women and missions is so fraught with contradictions that it is impossible to make a critical synthesis, one can only describe the conflicting constituent elements. We will continue to move back and forth among these three positions, in an attempt to understand the phenomenon of cultural imperialism: the cultural domination of one region or country, or sex, over another and the price middle-class women in the church must pay to achieve their own liberation.

One can find major *parallels* between the effects of missions on their converts and the effects of Christianity on its female adherents. In both cases, the ideology or rhetoric is one of equality and possibility and liberation. Yet the reality has been one of institutional forms and value assumptions which reinforce inferior status and identity. As the rhetoric was translated into the images and assumptions and policies of male-dominated western civilization, it was internalized by western women and by non-Americans in such a way that they believed in, assented to, their own essential inferiority and made their loyalties those of the dominant males and/or the missionaries.

There are also significant *differences* between western women and colonized peoples. U.S. Protestant women involved in missions have come from middle- to upper-middle-class backgrounds and have been relatively well-educated. In addition, although their status has been inferior to that of men at home *and* abroad, they have functioned at least in part as agents of an ideology which was alien to the ways of non-westerners and assumed to be superior.

The women who went abroad as missionaries in the latter half of the nineteenth and the early part of the twentieth centuries were well-educated for their time; they represented the elite of their era, at least educationally and sometimes economically as well. Although some women struggled to obtain their education and attain their cherished goal of becoming a missionary, others came from well-established families. Eliza Jane Gillett Bridgman, in 1845 the first unmarried American woman sent to China, married Dr. Elijah Coleman Bridgman, the first American male missionary to go to China, within two months of her arrival. During the last ten years of her life she was a widow, and during this period she established a school funded through her own private income.[44] Mary Sharp had sufficient independent income to enable her to stay on in Liberia in defiance of the Woman's Foreign Missionary Society of the Methodist Episcopal Church, which was displeased that she had established mostly male congregations and demanded that she return to the States.[45]

Other women missionaries came from the families of pastors and academics, where women's aspirations to education and medical training were at least considered valid. Furthermore, regardless of their class origins, women missionaries frequently lived in conditions of wealth relative to the living standards of those with whom they worked. As China missionary Mary Porter Gamewell pointed out at the turn of the century, "even in providing ordinary comfort we give the impression of wealth. . . . The money we use seems to stand between us and the people we would reach, by force of the bad motives it creates."[46]

Beyond the parallels and differences in the situations of women and colonized people there are the conflicting elements, the contradictions. Some women missionaries felt strong identification with the country where they lived and the people among whom they worked; others retained a distance bordering on disdain. "Christ died even for them. Yes, for the very lowest," remarked one Methodist missionary of the Mexicans with whom she worked.[47] Lochie Rankin wrote that "living among Chinese unfits us for intercourse with society. . . . It is quite enough to make hermits of us."[48] Mary Sharp communicated her sense of superiority to her charges; her tombstone near Monrovia reads, "Mary A. Sharp, 1837–1914. Erected to Honor the Memory of Our 'Mammy' By Her Boys and the Kroo Church."[49]

Some women who became missionaries may have acted as agents of foreign domination. In the name of saving souls some may have hastened the process of Americanization or helped reinforce class distinctions in the societies where they worked. Some may have provided upward mobility for only the select few with whom they worked. Yet that is not the whole story. Missionaries also have many accomplishments to their credit.

In societies where women were treated as little better than domesticated animals, missionaries offered an image of their being equal before God. Missionaries rescued girl babies from threats of infanticide and staffed orphanages to raise them. In places where girl children were sold into slavery, concubinage, or marriage, the missionaries spoke out condemning these practices and worked to change supportive legislation and custom.[50] Missionaries went to teach women and girls, defying the norms which denied such opportunities.[51] Missionaries in girls' schools experimented with educational methods ahead of their time. Missionaries brought changes in public practices of sanitation and hygiene.

Those examples are fairly clear, and positive. Other examples raise as many questions as they answer. In particular, what contribution did the specific orientation of women missionaries and women's societies to the needs of women and girls in foreign lands make to changing their status? In the case of China, missionaries on local and regional levels agitated against the practice of footbinding; yet they also supported Methodist Chiang Kai-shek in his 1927 suppression of the Communists, and his subsequent reactionary reversals of the gains women had made in the early Twenties. Were missionaries in other countries also simultaneously both helping and hindering women in their struggle to lead lives as full human beings?

Where does this leave us? With a tale of contradictions, with women alternately and simultaneously in the roles of victims and victimizers, colonized and colonizers, oppressed and oppressors. The story of U.S. Protestant women, and even the story of the work of women's missionary societies, is one of women who suffered from internal domination by male standards and structures and laws, unable to make decisions which affected their lives or even to spend the money accumulated through their efforts, and who finally succumbed to the nonconfrontational patterns of "soft feminism." Yet these same women helped spread the Gospel of the American Way of Life outside our borders. Although U.S. Protestant women did not make many mission board policies or articulate the supporting rationale, in their faithful implementation of policy and ideology were they not in fact agents of U.S. cultural imperialism?

A Concluding Assessment

There remain many unresolved questions which demand research and reflection going beyond the scope of this essay. Much more work remains to be done on the ties between religious and economic expansion, in order to answer such questions as: Haven't the missionaries, men as well as women, sometimes stood in opposition to foreign expansion and economic exploitation of the people they lived among and loved? Has their commitment to a gospel of love, even with its frequent implications of a practice of nonviolence, always worked in favor of the *status quo*? Did not the missionaries, in their work and in their encouraging presence, sometimes offer hope to the hopeless and the courage to survive in the face of overwhelming odds? Did not their introduction of new religious sects lead to a proliferation rather than to a consolidation of religious activity? And didn't this proliferation hamper efforts to develop a unified authority, foreign or indigenous, which would control the society and keep people in long-assigned places? And, finally, how have the effects of the ties between missionary activity and economic expansion of U.S. interests been similar, how different, in Asia, Africa, and Latin America?

Other open questions relate specifically to *women* in missions and the work of women missionaries. For example, were women freer from the ties between commerce, diplomacy, and religion than were the men? Were their perspectives less chauvinist, did they feel real equality with those in other lands sooner than men? And why did the activity of U.S. Protestant women overseas affect so little the status of women in the United States, within and outside the churches?

The information thus far available about the relation between women and missions and imperialism leads one to conclude that, when foreign economic interests are significant for a country, as has been increasingly the case for the United States around the globe, then the *primary* effects of religious activity originating from that foreign power will be, with varying degrees of effectiveness, to strengthen its influence. So, finally, women who in the United States were in part kept in their place through the church's sacralization of women's inferiority, have functioned outside the country to extend that *status quo*, including those parts that kept them in a less-than-equal position.

There is no question that these women accomplished many good works, that they endured much suffering and self-sacrifice, that when they went out hoping to preach the Gospel and save souls they made good use of one of the few options open to them for taking significant responsibility in the life of the churches. Whatever the intent, the basic effect of these missions, and the work of the missionaries both male and female, seems to have been to confuse the "christianizing" and the "civilizing" (or Americanizing) tasks in such a way that western patterns have been developed, values inculcated, ties of loyalty to sending bodies established. As a result, when there was conflict between the interests of the United States and a given other culture, as has already happened in both Cuba and China, those exposed to missionary activity endured that conflict within themselves and sometimes opted for the U.S.-related religious loyalty over the indigenous national or secular loyalty.

That is the tentative historical assessment. Perhaps equally important for us today is to discern what, if any, contemporary parallels we face.

Through the current interaction of issues one wonders whether present-day feminists within the U.S. churches do not run similar risks of being incorporated into an existing power structure, becoming oppressors in the process of achieving liberation. Greater opportunities for upward mobility, for interesting and responsible work, are opening for some women, especially well-educated white women. Those of us who work in the so-called social services, including the ministry, may find ourselves in the position of our sisters a century and half a century ago. We may, however, find or create some loopholes or breathing spaces, so that our own options are broader. We may also perform some good works, improve the situation of some individuals "less fortunate" than we. Yet, in the end, we may find that unless we challenge the fundamental class and hierarchical basis of our society we will have failed to bring about any basic or lasting change. We may even, wittingly or not, have prevented such change by beguiling some persons into thinking that because their work seemed more meaningful, or the particular conditions of their individual lives were better, then the problem of cultural and economic domination had been resolved.

I say to myself and to my sisters as we work for our future, beware lest others in even more vulnerable situations than we foot the bill for our seeming liberation!

NOTES

1. Two recent books deal with the history of women in missions, and have been helpful resources for writing this essay. R. Pierce Beaver's *All Loves Excelling: American Protestant Women in World Mission* (Grand Rapids, Mich.: William B. Eerdmans Publishing Company, 1968) is a systematic, comprehensive, historical study of Protestant women in missions; he concentrates primarily on the period from 1800 to 1925. Elaine Magalis' *Conduct Becoming to a Woman: Bolted Doors and Burgeoning Missions* (New York: Women's Division, Board of Global Ministries, The United Methodist Church, 1973) tells the story of women in the five constituent denominations of the present-day United Methodist Church; she concentrates primarily on women in overseas missions, although she also has chapters on women in national missions and women as pastors. These two authors have consulted old records, personal reminiscences and board reports, to piece together some of the hidden history of our foremothers. But even their useful work is only a beginning—much more research and reflection still lies ahead in this area of women's history.
2. Beaver, pp. 112–113.
3. U.S. economic, military, and diplomatic interventions around the globe have triggered increasingly vigorous opposition and caused a re-examination of long-cherished assumptions in this country, especially during the past decade. As a result, there has been a virtual explosion of analyses of distribution of wealth and power in the so-called Third World, and of the mechanisms of exploitation exercised by western capitalism, especially that located in the United States and in multinational corporations. Only recently have the further ties, those with less explicit economic bases, also been subject for discussion. Although there have been occasional essays on the particular topic of religion and imperialism—a few in English; most in French or Spanish or Portuguese—there is not yet any comprehensive study equivalent to Beaver's work on women and missions.
4. Quoted from Julius W. Pratt, *Expansionists of 1898: The Acquisi-*

tion of Hawaii and the Spanish Islands (1936; reprint ed. Chicago: Quadrangle Paperback, 1964), p. 300.

5. *North American Protestant Ministries Overseas, 1970,* quoted from Rick Edwards, "Protestant Missions: Preliminary Notes," *Nacla Newsletter,* December 1970, p. 19.
6. William R. Read, Victor Monterroso, and Harmon A. Johnson, *Latin American Church Growth,* quoted from Edwards, "Protestant Missions," p. 21.
7. Beaver, p. 11.
8. So far as I know, except for occasional sentence or paragraph asides, nothing has been written previously which looks closely at the interrelation between the three elements: women, missions, and imperialism.
9. Beaver, p. 52.
10. *Ibid.*, pp. 83–84.
11. Winifred Matthews, *Dauntless Women* (New York: Friendship Press, 1947), p. 12.
12. Beaver, p. 52.
13. *Annual Report* of the American Board for 1824, quoted from Beaver, p. 67.
14. Beaver, p. 85.
15. Magalis, p. 28.
16. *Ibid.*, p. 38.
17. Beaver, p. 107.
18. *Ibid.*, p. 151.
19. *Ibid.*, pp. 121–122.
20. *Ibid.*, p. 101.
21. *Ibid.*, pp. 172–174.
22. Magalis, p. 52.
23. Recurrent phrase in the annual reports of Mrs. Skidmore from the New York branch of the Woman's Foreign Missionary Society of The Methodist Episcopal Church for 1926, quoted in Magalis, p. 47.
24. Beaver, p. 179.
25. Magalis, p. 52.
26. *Ibid.*, p. 52.
27. *Ibid.*, p. 54.
28. *Ibid.*, p. 54.
29. *Ibid.*, p. 47.
30. *Ibid.*, p. 47.
31. *Ibid.*, p. 16.
32. See Beverly Harrison's article, "Sexism and the Contemporary Church: When Evasion Becomes Complicity," in this volume.

33. James O'Connor, "The Meaning of Economic Imperialism," in *Readings in U.S. Imperialism,* eds. K. T. Fann and Donald C. Hodges (Boston: Porter Sargent, 1971), p. 40.
34. Han Suyin, *A Mortal Flower* (New York: G. P. Putnam's Sons, 1965), pp. 264–265.
35. Quoted from "Georgia Methodism and Coca-Cola," Institute for Southern Studies, Atlanta, Ga. Circulated at the General Conference of the United Methodist Church held in Atlanta in April 1972.
36. *Christian Work in Latin America* (New York: The Missionary Education Movement, 1916), pp. 51-52.
37. Beaver, p. 125.
38. Magalis, p. 60.
39. Mrs. J. T. Gracey, *Eminent Missionary Women* (New York: Eaton and Mains, 1898), p. 142.
40. Beaver, p. 54.
41. Magalis, p. 128.
42. Figures on missionaries quoted from Edwards, p. 19; figures on Peace Corps Volunteers obtained in telephone conversation with Peace Corps, Boston office, November 1972.
43. Edwards, p. 21.
44. Beaver, p. 84.
45. Magalis, pp. 56-57.
46. *Ibid.,* p. 49.
47. *Ibid.,* p. 41.
48. *Ibid.,* p. 52.
49. *Ibid.,* p. 57.
50. For example, in 1890 Dr. Nancy Monell was responsible for presenting to the colonial government in India a petition to raise the legal marriageable age of girls to fourteen years; she based her argument on medical grounds. She was partially successful; the age was raised to twelve. Beaver, p. 134.
51. For example, Beaver (p. 99) notes that Baptist Lottie Moon, in her school at Tengchow, was "hampered by the prevailing hostility to the education of girls."

SEXISM AND THE CONTEMPORARY CHURCH:

When Evasion Becomes Complicity

Beverly Wildung Harrison

In the preface to his remarkable book *At the Edge of History,* William Irwin Thompson makes a comment which is comforting to anyone who takes on a topic of the scope set by the title of this essay. He says: "One can say almost anything about human culture now and it will be true, for everything is going on at once . . . ."[1] I agree with Thompson. In such a situation, I am aware that generalization is easy, and that a case can be made for nearly any thesis. But it also becomes clear, when everything is going on at once, that what we *choose* to notice about what is going on reveals much about who we are. The moralist's old claim that understanding itself is a moral act gains fresh credence once again. When everything is happening, the decision to understand or not is a moral act and it makes very good sense to put the question of responsibility in such a situation. It makes sense, in short, to consider questions about "evasion" and "complicity."

My topic has two principal terms—sexism and the contemporary churches—and a moral component. It will be the burden of my argument to make clear the depth of the moral component in this issue: the question of evasion and complicity. In order to get to my major thesis, however, I must first locate and delimit the two key terms. I will come to the question of complicity directly only at the end.

Sexism

Sexism is a term recently coined. It arises out of the consciousness of the present women's movement, and like all such terms born of human movements and articulated to denote the ills which gave rise to them, it has a more evaluative than descriptive intent. It is obviously not a neutral term. I use the term intentionally, and endorse its evaluative force. I take it for granted that ours is a sexist society and that our churches are sexist; I assume that sexism is wrong; i.e., that we ought to act against it. I hope you will bear with me briefly while I justify that judgment.

I mean by *sexism* an ethos and a value structure, and the formal and informal social patterns which support that ethos and value structure in our social world. *Formal patterns* of sexism are those institutionalized in law and procedural rules. *Informal patterns* are those sustained by custom and emotional preference. This ethos and value system of sexism, sustained by some formal and many informal patterns, is aimed at maintaining the arrangements between male and female which have been passed down to us in our social world. I am fully aware that an observer, claiming dispassion, might object that what I call *sexism* is really nothing other than differentation of social roles between male and female. Such a dispassionate observer might argue that sex-role differentiation is as old as human history, as natural as the air we breathe, and that it must be highly functional for human society since it has survived until now. Obviously I do not accept this version of the functionalist's argument. Societies, I admit, have a way of wanting to survive—to hang in there and not fall apart. They tolerate what they tolerate because it *feels* like it is functional to survival. Change makes all of us feel insecure. But most societies actually do come apart, and as often as not they do so because they keep insisting that something is "natural" or "inevitable" or "desirable" well past the point when what is done is any longer humanly tolerable, much less wise.

In any case, what makes the differentiation between male and female social roles which we have sexist and therefore wrong is the inequity of the human identity which that social differentiation between the sexes distributes. *Male* is male and means certain things in our social world; *female* is female and means certain largely other things. But, to use a shorthand formula which best describes the problem—one I borrow from Elizabeth Janeway[2]—what is male, according to prevailing distribution, is defined by "world." *World* is man's place. Female is defined by a more restricted "sphere"—woman's place. Woman's place varies from society to society; it is whatever sector of man's world a given society has carved out for her. Although in our present situation woman's place differs radically from culture to culture, it is always "place" and never "world."

We know now, thanks to our hard-won historical sense, that the limits set for us by the map of our social roles also set the limits of the individual identity which each of us can develop. Thus "man's world, woman's place" as the general formula for identity distribution has had immense consequences. We are very wary of speaking any more of the nature of man. Man's nature, we know, has become whatever it is that man has done, and whatever accrued to his identity in the doing of it. Woman's nature is whatever she has done, and what has accrued to her identity in the doing of that. Ergo—man's nature is broader, more wide-ranging than woman's. And, we should add, it will remain so, until what is female is defined with reference to "world," as male now is.

The moral onus of sexism can be seen if you pause to consider what is entailed when an individual male is told that he is a defective male and what an individual woman is told when she is charged with being a defective female. Both individuals can be deeply wounded, at the psychological level, by such an accusation. There is no difference in that regard. But the male so charged is told that he is not a *man*. The woman is told that she is not *feminine*. That is a very different thing. In the accusation directed to the male there is a dominant note which suggests *omission*. There is always some suggestion implied that the male in question has failed to go forth and meet the world as he ought to have done. The omission is usually one of act or initiative, and the charge suggests some failure in the arena of activity. The female, on the other hand, hears the charge of defective feminity differently. The charge will most often arise because she has been guilty of a *commission*. She will have said something she should not have said, aspired to do or have done something which she should not have done. In short, she has crossed that invisible but powerful boundary out of her territory. The charge of being "not feminine," I submit, is aimed at thwarting initiative. Its message is: "Go back."

Since sexism is a social phenomenon, however, this problem can best be seen on the social level. The inequality of identity which sexism distributes is obvious at that level. Until the advent of Gay

Liberation—which as a *movement* is clearly dependent upon the ideological space carved out by the women's movement—no movement involving men could ever have been discredited as "unmanly." However, society has a built-in ideological weapon available against any women's social movement: "unfeminine!" Women's movements have an ideological fragility that has nothing at all to do with the fragility of woman's nature. That fragility is inherent in the uneven identity distribution which results from our social differentiations of male and female. It is, in short, inherent in sexism itself!

It is true, of course, that this uneven distribution of identity implicit in sexism has been widely and actively protested only in the modern period. That is because historical awareness is its presupposition. The glib charge is often made that the present women's movement is a white, middle-class affair; for the most part, that charge is true. While I cannot do justice to all the dimensions of that contention—nor to the ideological purposes of those who use it as a put-down—I would point out that *all* radical consciousness presupposes the social conditions of the middle-class world. Widespread historical consciousness, as a mode of self-understanding, is a product of the bourgeois world. Bourgeois society, for better or worse, has carried the germ of historical self-understanding in its wake and has planted it widely enough to reap the whirlwind against itself. All the spokesmen who have challenged the inevitabilities of our social world in behalf of the victims of that presumed inevitability must stand in continuity with that consciousness; or they could not be aliens to it, as they are.

The questions which the women's movement has raised, and which stem from the collapse of a sense of inevitability regarding man's world and woman's place, may be put well or they may be put badly. They may be articulated fairly or unfairly in terms of the historical record—but they are there and had better be faced without resort to cheap tactics of evasion.

Nevertheless, I, for one, concede that the women's movement is subject to a temptation born of the widespread and long-standing nature of sexism. That temptation is to allow the question of *why these things should be* to become an overwhelming preoccupation. It is understandable that women who have suddenly become aware, in the deepest reaches of their being, that their every assumption about themselves has been planted by a social system they did not—and now need not—assent to, should ask *why*. But sexism is so old and of such long standing that no univocal answer is adequate. Women have spun some quite specious theories in seeking for a simple answer. This search for a simple, single social hypothesis has put some of us in a conspiratorial frame of mind.

In my view, the *why* question is a complicated one, and one we ought not to press too far back; when we ask it, it should be by way of understanding our historical present, the better to change it. Social sex-role differentiation is obviously of long standing. It is rooted in biology and in earliest cultural patternings. For most people over most of the earth, most of the time, birth and social location have been destiny. Most human beings have made the best of that because they had no other choice. This has been especially so of women.

Having said that, however, I want to go on to speak to the *why* question within the framework of that historical present which is the context of many of us women: the dominant American culture, and in the churches which until recently have both reflected and molded that dominant culture. This brings me finally to the second term in my topic: the contemporary churches.

The Churches

Because of my own historical location and because I think the story of the women's movement and its relation to the dominant American churches of the nineteenth century—what we sometimes call "the mainline Protestant churches"—has received insufficient attention, I want to aim my generalizations there. What I have to say about sexism and the churches will *not* apply in the same degree to three other Christian groups in America.

What I have to say will *not* apply directly to those churches and sects that are the Christian home of the very poor; nor to those indigenous churches developed by persons of color. The lines of caste and class in America exclude one from the niceties of observing the distinctions of social role operative in the dominant culture. In groups cut off by class, and especially in those excluded by caste, survival is the name of the game; under those conditions male and female do what they can, and what they must, without undue concern for social role. The patterns of sexism of which I will speak do not apply there *unless* and *until* these churches take the turn and become channels of upward social mobility.

Nor does what I have to say apply to those churches and religious groups which, for whatever reasons, have resisted the encroachments of modernity through stern ideological resistance to critical and historical consciousness. These churches have survived and are flourishing in America, and their trump card against the women's movement is that they need make no room for it. The women's movement can be dealt with easily in these churches, under the univocal rubric of "sin." There, women can find a place only if they settle for the strategy and tactics which—as I will point out—women in the nineteenth century adopted in the mainline, dominant churches.

Thirdly, my remarks do not apply directly to those churches, of which the Roman Catholic is the major example, where orders and ordination are still principally understood in terms of public sacramental mediation. The patterns of sexism in these churches vary slightly from those of the dominant American tradition. In these churches, the patterns of sexism are legitimated at a symbolic level so potent that women struggling in them need to be forearmed with a special understanding of the emotional load their demands for change carry. Where *patriarchy* and the *public* mediation of grace are deeply entwined, there are very special problems which I cannot address here.

The dominant churches—those which marshaled and channeled the cultural hegemony of what we loosely call WASP society, those in which ordination or orders are chiefly understood in terms of preaching and teaching—were, I submit, deeply affected by the women's movement of the nineteenth century. It is one of the major characteristics of these churches that they do not want to understand how deeply they were changed by it.

In order to understand how this is so, we must pause briefly to remind ourselves of the accounts of nineteenth-century feminism which are now being given under the impact of the new feminism—the feminism that emerged in the 1960s.

The Old Feminism

The feminism of the nineteenth century—what I will call here "the old feminism"—arose, as we know, as an element in that Pandora's box of social reform which characterized America in that century. The old feminism's rise was closely interwined with the abolitionist movement, and surely would not have found its initial, *radical* shape without the struggle to free the slaves. Like all impulses to reform during this period, it was initially generated by Christian conscience, and understood itself to be an expression of it.

Angelina Grimké, that heroine of new feminists, is perhaps the archetypical figure in the development of radical Christian consciousness regarding woman's place in society. In an important study, one which nicely foretells the ambivalences and fate of nineteenth-century feminism in the churches, Dorothy Bass has traced the debates between Angelina Grimké and Catherine Beecher regarding abolitionism and woman's place.[3]

Grimké's radical consciousness about the role of women stands, as we look back upon it today, an astonishing example of cultural transcendence. Grimké had an incredible grasp of human possibility and a glorious vision of the Kingdom of God as well as a profound sensibility to the dynamics of evil. Under other circumstances she might have been the finest theologian of her age! But the fate that awaited her in relation to the church—the same fate that awaited each of those few women who understood the radicality of *social* equality—was derision. Her work in behalf of abolition of slavery caused her, almost literally, to be driven from the dominant church. Derided by clergy, shunned by other Christians, including women, she left the dominant church and became a Quaker. Among the Quakers she was to discover that the commitment to the abolition of slavery did not extend to women. The derision she endured in behalf of abolitionism was nothing compared to what she encountered when she extended her public critique to sexism.

The clear response of the churches to the initial challenge generated by the women's movement was foreshadowed in Grimké's fate. Radical feminism survived, but under increasing duress, and with ever-growing alienation from the churches. The story of the churches' response is so obvious and so predictable that most spokeswomen for the new feminism can find no line of connection between their own reality and the dynamics of church life in the intervening period. The churches did indeed, by ostracism and denunciation, inoculate themselves against the *radical* feminist possibility.

Yet it is a mistake of the highest order to assume that the women's movement was successfully driven from the churches. The inoculation against radical feminism was successful only up to a point. The radical feminist ideology, with its demand for the full social equality of women, was indeed excluded; but that ideology was only the tip of a social iceberg. Radical feminism survived, carried by individuals whom we rightly admire as examples of social transcendence. It was an heroic consciousness, and we have reason today to be grateful for the sacrifice and price that was paid by women who bore it. Still, the women's movement ran deeper. What generated it was social reality. The movement was a response, albeit not a fully conscious response, to social forces and, as such, it could not be turned back.

If the society (and with it, the majority of women) could not tolerate the claims that radical feminism laid upon it, many, many women could, and did, do the next best thing. They accepted the social dictates of woman's place, and decided with a vengeance to take responsibility for the sphere that had been granted them.

What many women, even those fearful of radical feminism, were responding to, I submit, was a subtly encroaching split between the interpersonal and the public sphere which an incipient industrial system was bringing on. At a very deep level, women perceived that split as a threat to the things they cared about. They sensed their responsibility to rectify what was taking place. If women were not ready to hear the likes of Angelina Grimké, that proponent of what I am calling "radical feminism," they were prepared to come to grips with another feminist possibility, the one to which Catharine Beecher gave early expression. They would struggle to assure that feminine values survived in a world growing ever more inimical to them. They would, if you will, "feminize" the ever more remote public world. They would aim their efforts and energies at those for whom no one could deny them responsibility—other women, children, the sick and disabled. They would, and they did.

If Catharine Beecher, that nineteenth-century prophet of what we may term "soft feminism,"[4] penned her appeals to women and obeyed the social dictates by having her speeches read in public by a man, her followers—making good upon her ideology—carried things so far that they even learned to speak publicly for themselves. They followed "soft feminism" where it led, and it led to some very unlikely places indeed!

Predictably, the battles for acceptance which these soft feminists got involved in were very rough. These women were not rewarded for their greater willingness to stay within the boundary of their proper sphere of influence; nor were they appreciated for the greater reasonableness of the demands they made under the aegis of "soft feminism." But their persistence was as remarkable as their patience.

I have neither the competence nor the space to trace in detail the story of the women's struggles, nor to give an adequate account of their relative success in the battle to carry the values of nurturance and personal care and concern into the remote social world. However, that story is now, finally, being reconstructed by many historians.

An important chapter in the story, as it relates to one major aspect of church life, is R. Pierce Beaver's history of the rise of women's foreign mission boards, *All Loves Excelling*.[5] If Dr. Beaver's account falters badly in his effort to explain what happened to the women's movement, it at least has the virtue of giving us details of a struggle within the churches which most have long since forgotten or do not wish to know.

While my own sympathies with "soft feminism" are obviously born out of a desire and effort to understand more than to justify, I do not think that we can minimize its victories, especially in changing the ethos of the dominant churches. It is hard to believe today, for example, some of the facts of which Dr. Beaver and others remind us.[6] For example, that in 1910 one-third of the over-one-thousand American doctors practicing medicine as missionaries in foreign lands were women (there were 350 of them). Or that as late as 1930—that year which marks the statistical watershed in the collapse of feminism[7]—two-thirds of the missionaries in some of the mainline churches were women.

The successes of "soft feminism," I submit, can be measured even better by the more surprising fact that in the dominant churches, most of the *formal* barriers to the full participation of women fell in the wake of a women's movement which did not even have the removal of those formal barriers as its major goal.

That last bastion of institutionalized sexism—ordination or clergy status—gave way, over a long period and in varied battles, because women's social base within the churches had become strong enough to give the lie to the claim of female incompetence even in this holy of holies. As I read the record, battles over the ordination of women in the mainline churches, while vigorous in some quarters, were for the most part surprising not for their vehemence, but for the relative lack of it.

Certainly, some of these successes of "soft feminism" have to be credited to the minimal threat which the soft-feminist ideology posed to the symbolic center of the churches' life. Women did not, for the most part, aspire to the preaching and teaching roles that were at the cultic center of these churches. Had many women done so, the story of formal institutional adjustment might have been quite different. Had women not been committed so deeply to their specially appointed tasks, they might not have fared so well at the level of formal, institutionalized sexism. As it was, since they were willing to go nearly anywhere and to undertake anything their "place" required, since they were willing to do jobs which men often were unwilling to do, and to make greater sacrifices, they were not turned away.

The debits or weaknesses of soft-feminist ideology are perhaps too obvious to need comment, but two seem important to observe. The first is that the ideology of "soft feminism" required even the most energetic and courageous of these women to consent to the thesis that they had a "special nature." That consent was not at all devastating in its initial consequences. For "soft feminism" pushed many women out of the home and into the public sphere, and women did not let their self-accepted definition limit their undertakings at very many points. They had much to learn, and they learned it. Yet at one fatal point, in the churches of which I am speaking, "soft feminism" could not penetrate. In these churches the cultic center—preaching and teaching—is also the sphere which symbolizes the human rationality that faith involves. The ordained office in these churches involves a role specialization which places the responsibility for full critical intelligence upon the clergy—that is the clergy's special province. What "soft feminism" could not do in these churches was to legitimate women at that key point where modern identity demands legitimation—in terms of the power of intellect and critical intelligence. What this feminism could not do, in short, was to give to the women involved their full intellectual self-respect! The story which needs telling in this connection is the fate of women in relation to the theological education of these churches. Unfortunately, I have no space to tell it here.

The second deficit of "soft feminism" that needs to be noted was its inability to inoculate women against that deep nemesis inherent in feminism as a social movement: the charge of "deficient femininity." I have already mentioned this problem. It follows that any ideology of feminism which does not set its sights upon the definition of "feminine" in terms of "place" cannot shake free of that peculiar vulnerability which is inherent in its social location. To accept self-definition in terms of place means to internalize the boundary which is itself the problem. That internalization of boundary accounts for the peculiar ambivalence of "soft feminism," and its extreme fragility as a social movement. In the face of the charge of defective feminity, many soft feminist turned back. They did so with a whimper rather than with a bang, for loud noises have no room in "woman's place." Discouraged, dispirited, disappointed—they often cried and withdrew in mute frustration. To fight was to remove themselves from the very ground on which they stood.

The Debacle of Feminism

Let me add, emphatically, that I do not call attention to these deficiencies and weaknesses of "soft feminism" with any intent to give credence to the widespread assumption that the debacle of the old feminism—and it was a complete debacle—rests with the personal shortcomings of these soft-feminist women. Some prevailing historical interpretations suggest that feminism's decline is best accounted for by the strategic error women made in focusing too narrowly upon the goal of political suffrage; or that feminism failed, inundated by the eccentricities of militant women.

The first debacle of feminism, I submit, is better understood as inherent in the dynamics of the advanced industrial socioeconomic system. Feminism arose as a response to the challenges of rising industrialization. Women responded to the ever-clearer split between the interpersonal sphere and the growing public sphere of technical rationality that was inherent in the rising socioeconomic system. They did so out of a desire to maintain interpersonal values and humane meaning in our social world. But the dynamics of industrialization and the conditions of technical rationalization outstripped the energies and resources of beleaguered women, as they did the energies and efforts of many men. These women understood no more fully than did the men around them what was occurring, or what might be at stake, but their grasp of the problem was not less clear. They knew something fateful was happening.

I have referred to "the first debacle" of feminism and taken it for granted that what I mean by this term is clear. I am constantly brought up short, however, by the realization that outside the circles where the new feminism has penetrated, awareness of this debacle hardly exists. In American society generally, and conspicuously in the mainline churches, there is hardly any awareness that the march of women into the public world was turned back on all fronts in the period between 1910 and 1965, and turned back with a vengeance. For that reason, a further word about this great reversal is in order here. I have already insisted that "soft feminism" successfully permeated the Protestant churches. It goes without saying that the collapse of *formal* barriers to women's fuller participation, both in these churches and in the wider society, itself helped to create an impression—by this time an illusion—that the battles for women's rights had been won. Until the advent of the new feminism, the most conspicuous characteristic of the dominant culture was its easy conscience on the subject of women. Mistaking the sphere of admitted greater *personal* freedom of women for that of *social* emancipation, the dominant culture failed even to be interested in what was really taking place.

How else does one explain the shock and misunderstanding that often greet the new feminism? How many innocently ask: What *are* women angry about? What *do* women want? Have not the barriers fallen? Are not more women, better educated than ever before, working outside their homes, free to come and go and do what they like? Even those few social scientists who have tried to point to the real indicators—the socioeconomic ones—have gone unheeded.[8] It comes as a shock to most people to learn that the incomes of working women in relation to those of men have been steadily worsening over four decades. Many are surprised to learn that an ever smaller percentage of the professional and semiprofessional roles in this society are occupied by women, and that this downward trend is clear-cut over forty years. These statistics are but the gross indicators of a deeper story.

I have already offered my account of the causes of the feminist debacle. What needs to be added is a word about the *dynamics* of the reversal, in both church and society. Regardless of whatever account interpreters offer of the causes of the debacle, most now agree that the trend of feminism began to wane even before the First World War. Both world wars accelerated the destruction of feminism. We know now, of course, that our twentieth-century wars have had much to do with speeding up the dynamics and development of the American socio-industrial system. These wars have also had a lot to do with triggering the desperate search for human meaning in the interpersonal sphere. In any case, it is clear that by the 1920s many women were willing to settle for their newfound *personal* freedom; they were willing to enjoy that and would not press further. Their mother's struggles had ceased to matter—had, in fact, even ceased to *make sense* to them. Their mood, of course, was not much different from that of the men, as the images of the Roaring Twenties attest.

Then came the Great Depression. Women, with a fragile and fading toehold on social equality, were, you may be sure, very hard hit by it. Although World War II saw women once again welcomed in every role, the end of the war found many women willing to join with men in the headlong dash to privatization.

By the 1950s, all the trends which brought on the new feminism were well advanced. Technical rationality and its attendant bureaucratization had succeeded in sealing off the interpersonal worlds—now the province of home, family, friendship—from the public worlds of work and profession. "Woman's place" and "man's world" had come apart with a vengeance; but the consequences for women were not what you might expect. As many women have reminded us, far from losing status, the interpersonal sphere now took on a status and an emotional importance that it could not have had previously.[9] Family life, sexual intimacy, interpersonal relations—the whole web of values which makes up what we call "the cult of the nuclear family"—took on an importance and an emotional valence which they had never previously held. Woman became the high priestess of the cult of the personal world and had to carry the immense burden of success or failure there. The stakes were high, for failure there could less and less be compensated for elsewhere. The present discontent of women is certainly as much a protest against this difficult, emotion-laden responsibility (a responsibility which neither male nor female is adequate to bear alone) as it is active demand for wider access to "man's world."

The Contemporary Churches: Evasion

What was going on in the mainline churches during this period is fully analogous to what went on within the dominant culture. As the split between the interpersonal and public spheres widened, women who had given their lives to fight that split grew less and less able to cope with it. Armed initially with immense common sense and fairness, and a preference for the personal mode bred of their special place, they could not navigate the niceties of bureaucratization and technical rationalization as readily as do men.

Churches tolerated the incumbency of the older feminists until they retired, but then they were replaced by men. It was clear to the leadership of these churches that the men were more competent to do the task at hand. On the mission field, the pressure for indigenization of churches was responded to, first of all, by giving male nationals those roles which women had previously staked out. (American males, you may be sure, were slower to turn pulpit and lectern over to the nationals!). At home, where women had won belated professional status in the church as Christian educators, this field too eventually was "upgraded"; i.e., turned over to assistant ministers who were men. This was, after all, but one example of a widespread trend which saw all of the formerly "feminine" professions bureaucratized, rationalized, and taken over by men. Social work, along with elementary and secondary education, suffered the same fate. (First the men took over at the administrative level, and then, later, across the board.)

Furthermore, the demands of efficient and coordinated administration within the churches required the integration and homogenization of those agencies and organizations which women had founded and nurtured to carry out their mission of interpersonal penetration of the public sphere. Throughout this whole process, the dominant churches, armed with the knowledge that they had made way for women, that they had dropped *formal* barriers to their participation, found no reason to challenge their own easy conscience as these things took place.

These trends reduced an earlier substantive token representation of women to an all but nonexistent trickle. Yet this could plausibly be explained with reference to the individual idiosyncrasies of women, to their "peculiar" nature, and to man's "greater effectiveness." No need to ask, "Where have all the women gone?" And much less need to ask, "Why has it happened?"

Evasion was the order of the day. By the 1950s, when that temporary renaissance of dominant Protestant hegemony occurred, women of my generation who participated in the church's life did so primarily out of a professed interest in theology. Involvement in the church was for us a continuation of our liberal education aimed at personal fulfillment as an end in itself. We did not study theology out of desire, any longer, to have a full part in the church's mission. The word was out: working for the church was a lonely, frustrating road. Taking it, we feared, would lead to our ending up like those bitter, insecure women we all knew who had hung on a generation earlier. The men, of course, noticed this lack of seriousness on our part and used it as a further argument for turning back the clock and excluding women from theological education.[10]

When the new feminism arrived upon the scene in the 1960s, the *operative* exclusion of women from significant participation in the main-line churches was well advanced. *Formal* exclusion was not even needed. Surprisingly, however, the consciousness of new feminism generated almost overnight a constituency of women who began to show signs of wanting a full part in the life of the main-line churches at the very moment when it looked as though, for women, the jig was up. What these women found, of course, was a church in which the old feminism had so waned that role models were nonexistent. Support from other women, when there was any, was more likely to come from grandmothers than from mothers, from those in whom the dynamism of the old battle still smoldered.

The New Feminism

In what now appears an incredibly short time, the new feminism spawned a constituency whose consciousness shows signs of taking up where the old left off. In the last five years I have marked—month by month, and sometimes day by day—the dawning awareness in these young women of what *full* participation and *full* social equality means in the church. And I have seen these young women reject what few women of my generation would ever have dared to reject: the argument that their aspiration is a consequence of disordered feminity. I owe my own liberation, more deeply than to anything else, to the incredible privilege of sharing in the struggles of these younger women.

Even so, the future of the new feminism and its significance for the churches is tenuous in the extreme. I have avoided so far saying anything about the present state of those formerly dominant churches of the Protestant hegemony. It is obvious that the decade in which the new feminism emerged was also the decade when the social displacement of the mainline churches reached its zenith. The WASP became the symbol, par excellence, of the decaying order. The tenuous objectifications of the neo-orthodox theology bit the dust. And the Protestant clergyman became, even earlier than the Catholic priest, the cultural symbol of identity in crisis.

I have an immense sympathy for the plight of the contemporary Protestant clergyman, not least because my own analysis of what was happening to feminism forces me to the recognition that the social forces which routed feminism were the same ones that left the Protestant clergy exposed and vulunerable. While feminism was routed, the Protestant clergy continued to play a public, if increasingly informal and marginal, role within a society moving toward advanced industrialization. The split which decimated the women's movement was the same split that left the clergy standing almost alone within the public arena, proponents of the interpersonal world which the new order could not embody, but which, out of nostalgia, it wished not to forget. The Protestant clergyman became the court chaplain of the new order—expected to proclaim and protest (almost singlehandedly) the old values, but ever less able to do so with credibility.

I never cease to be amazed that few notice the similarities between the worst features of the dominant Protestant clergyman's stereotype and those characteristics thought to be intrinsic to woman's "nature"—i.e., sentimentality, indirectness of communication and moralizing, ambivalence and inconsistency of principle, preference for anecdotal rather than analytic thinking, fear of conflict, and a need to please and to be loved at any cost! Similarity of character, I submit, is largely similarity of social location. If clergymen survived their burdens in the new age for quite some time, as often as not it was because of the support system which women provided, for women were literally in a position to understand far better than most men the struggles of the clerical role in the churches of the Protestant hegemony.

But, in the decade of the 1960s, the dominant churches had little taste for the recognition of these realities. The women's movement, and the new feminism, presented itself to a leadership already burdened by the charges that followed upon its cultural displacement. Nostalgic for the old order of clear-cut cultural influence, flagellated on all sides simultaneously by charges of ineptitude because of lack of social impact, and faced with lack of interest and unconcern for what they had to say, Protestant clergy often experienced the women's movement as an irritant. They greeted it with petulant and faintly disapproving silence or with an anger seemingly born of recognition that the last vestiges of uncritical support and adulation for *their* social role might also collapse.

Like women, Protestant clergymen have been the victims of that misplaced personalism that sees their dilemmas more as a consequence of individual inadequacy than of systemic pressures not of their own making. A large degree of sympathy and understanding certainly is in order. Until now this understanding has been far more forthcoming from women than from the American male. But the problem is that the leadership of the churches is now poised precariously between nostalgia for the past and the discernment of fresh alternatives. And the outbreak of new and virulent forms of religiosity in American society bodes well to permit the leaders of these churches the opportunity to recover a sense of legitimacy and importance without having to come to terms with the new human movements and pressures—women's or any other. We seem to be poised between the option of a fresh line of march and a regression to the old role of cultural legitimation which hegemony made inevitable.

Mainline Protestantism, even if it chooses regression, will not, of course, regain the old hegemony. Too many other groups—including the upward-mobile evangelical churches—have got to the starting gate ahead of them. But there will be security in rushing back to fill the gap in legitimation of the new civil religion[11] which the advanced technological society requires. If the mainline churches move in this direction, that legitimation will be the more impressive, for there is still a great deal of power to split theological hairs left in these churches, and justification of the new civil religion will require considerable wit and ingenuity.

The alternative for the formerly dominant churches is far more difficult and requires not only intelligence but courage—courage which the guilt-ridden and nostalgic conscience of these communities will make difficult. The new marginality of these churches could be accepted and taken as a challenge. The ways could be found, by dint of energy and imagination, to something like the old believer's church model which was lost in the rising cultural hegemony of Protestantism. However, this model requires making good on one insight to which Protestantism has given lip service but clearly has never embodied: The church will be believed only through what it *does*; the evils it denounces must first be purged from its own life.

The reigning sociology of religion, itself spawned by dominant Protestant consciousness, has led us to believe that there is no rite of passage from "church-type" back to sectarian form; that is because analysis in the sociological mode stops with institutionalization, and organizational *change* has received hardly any attention. For my part, I believe a new line of march is possible—not probable, but possible—and that one of the reasons for this possibility is the emergence of the women's movement, making its claim upon these churches. Deeply aware of the limitations of the dominant patterns of specialization and professionalization in these churches, unwilling to accept the role of moral and spiritual guru to the dominant culture, and quite unnostalgic about the past, women are nevertheless willing to join men in a full ministry aimed at finding ways to embody communally the meaning of the Christian gospel. Such embodiment may help to make that gospel publicly comprehensible once again. Nothing else will do so. The name of the game for the formerly dominant churches is not, any longer, direct social power. It is communal comprehension. Not only are the old beliefs gone, but the old conditions of belief are gone as well.

Women are, in a way, the prototype of the conditions of any new spirituality. In the face of a Christian tradition sexist to the core, *we believe against belief*, quite consciously, and in full knowledge of what we are doing. Our problem is not simply to replicate the tradition—but to liberate it, to make it a vehicle of a human possibility it has not yet embodied. We know our faith requires a strategic departure in the direction of communal embodiment of faith, and we are not at all ashamed to say that what we need is what others need as well.

There is still much that needs to be said about these mainline churches. The battle line of the new feminism in these churches is far more subtle and shapeless than in those churches where other social conditions prevail. The absence of formal, institutionalized sexist barriers means that women in these churches must deal less directly with the politics of change than with the cultural arenas of consciousness and sensibility; we must awaken the slumbering consciences of those who feel that they have done their part and done enough.

Complicity?

I promised that at the end I would come directly to that moral component I included in my subject: the issue of evasion and complicity. Being a moralist by trade and inclination, I could write about these matters at length, but the essay is already overlong. I have clearly pressed my view that evasion of the issue of women's role has long been the order of the day within the churches. The failure to ask after the reasons for the eclipse of women is part and parcel of a larger failure—that of not understanding the fragile dialectic between the interpersonal and social spheres. As I noted at the outset, in a world where everything is happening all at once the moral component in what we choose to notice is clear. Consequently, in this situation evasion in understanding what is taking place needs to be understood as a psychic and social defense mechanism against the pressure to change. Such evasion is especially operative, as we know, among those who have power and therefore public responsibility. Their evasion on this issue is especially susceptible to the just charge of complicity.

But as one who tries to interpret the dynamics of the social world in terms of moral sensibility I must also add that evasion does not become complicity until and unless those who are damaged by the evasion put themselves on the line and press their claims. Evasion in the mainline churches on these matters is fast becoming complicity because such claims are being pressed. The moral conditions for complicity are set by a new women's movement which insists that it be taken seriously. Whether it is taken seriously and welcomed will be a very good index of whether the churches of the old hegemony can move forward to new possibility or will turn back to a safer, though duller, ground.

One final comment—this one aimed at those women who, like myself, have decided to take this evasion as a battle line, to test complicity. In both church and culture there are clear signs that a move is on to discredit the new feminism in much the same fashion as was the old. It is clear how deep our debt is to the old feminists. They won many battles for us. But because of conditions not of their making, we stand at a point not so very far removed from where they stood. They kept their place, and used that place well enough to learn that they were not by nature weak or fragile or intellectually deficient. They learned that their feminity was neither soiled nor distorted by their new responsibility. Without the evidence they embodied, we would not be where we are today. They pressed "woman's place" out until it almost reached the circumference of "man's world." But they could not fully circumnavigate the growing split. That split has widened still.

Much of what is worth knowing in the world is still best learned and nourished in what was woman's place. There are signs that many men are finally learning that as well. But if we owe these older sisters anything—and I think we do—it is to learn, through their suffering, the limits of place-staying. All the old weapons to keep us in our place are still around, and most of them are still credible. They will be used against us. Sisterhood, we say, is powerful. Let us hope it really is, for it will be tested as it has not yet been, not merely by evasion but by the powerful will in "man's world" to keep the human spheres from interpenetration.

NOTES

1. William Irwin Thompson, *At the Edge of History: Speculation on the Transformation of Culture* (New York: Harper & Row Colophon Books, 1972), p. ix.

2. Elizabeth Janeway, *Man's World, Woman's Place: A Study in Social Mythology* (New York: Delta Books, 1971). Ms. Janeway's work is by far the most adequate book available on the relation of social role to woman's identity. No discussion of the woman question which fails to come to grips with this issue can claim adequacy.

3. Dorothy Bass Fraser, "A Study in Abolitionism, Feminism, and Evangelical Religion: Catharine E. Beecher and Angelina E. Grimké 1837–1838" (M.A. thesis, Columbia University, 1972. Available from the author). Ms. Bass' study is crucial reading for those who would understand the dimensions of nineteenth century feminism.

4. The term "soft feminism" is one that is intended to encompass the perspectives of numerous nineteenth century women. Catharine Beecher was but one of many who, while rejecting full social equality for women, nevertheless articulated an ideology of women's role which ran counter to then prevailing definitions. The views of women like Catharine Beecher were ahead of their time in spite of their caution. Hence they did much to raise female self-respect and sense of worth. It should also be remembered that by the later Victorian period "soft feminism," spearheaded by women like Frances Willard, became oriented to direct political action.

5. R. Pierce Beaver, *All Loves Excelling* (Grand Rapids, Mich.: William B. Eerdmans Publishing Co., 1968).

6. See also, Marian Derby, "Where Have All the Women Gone?" (Mimeographed papers, World Division of the United Methodist Board of Missions, undated).

7. Ethel Alpenfels, "Women in the Professional World," in *American Women: The Changing Image*, ed. Beverly B. Cassara (Boston: Beacon Press, 1962).

8. *Ibid.* Cf. table added to U.S. Dept. of Labor Women's Bureau: *Fact Sheet on the Earnings Gap* (Pittsburgh: Know, Inc.); Cf. also Beverly Harrison, "Women's Liberation and Christian Faith" (manuscript, available from the author).

9. Janeway, *Man's World, Woman's Place.* Cf. also Betty Friedan, *The Feminine Mystique* (New York: W. W. Norton, 1963).

10. I have in my possession a few select unpublished documents, written in the 1950s, urging that women be excluded from theological education because of their lack of professional seriousness. I see no purpose here in citing authors by name, but the documents are available on request. Needless to say, these writers did not even raise the question of why women were "professionally unserious."

11. The "civil religion" of any society is best envisaged by considering that society's ideal as to what constitutes the good life and *who* symbolizes true success. Though I cannot here describe in detail what I take the contours of the "new civil religion" of advanced technological society to be, for purposes of my thesis, a key ingredient is the following: the civil religion accepts and legitimates a sharp distinction between interpersonal and public behavior. However, the personal virtues which are most valued are those which gear in most easily (i.e., with least cognitive dissonance) with successful public behavior. In this society these highest personal values include cooperativeness, loyalty to associates (cronyism), and providing well for one's family. The public virtues most highly valued include unflappability and coolness, expertise in application of technical rules. These two combined constitute what is called "rationality." Rationality also includes an appropriate self-consciousness about "public image" and an ability to project and manipulate images.

    While the outbreak of religiosity referred to above stands in some tension to this advanced industrial civil religion, these new outbreaks of religiosity will endure, in the long haul, only insofar as they adjust to the dominant civil religion ideal.

BIOGRAPHICAL SKETCHES OF CONTRIBUTORS

Biographical Sketches of Contributors

DOROTHY D. BURLAGE is presently a Ph.D. candidate in Clinical Psychology and Public Practice at Harvard University. One of the founders of the Women's Counseling and Resource Center in Cambridge, she has also worked with groups of separated and divorced persons in the Laboratory for Community Psychiatry of Harvard Medical School. She lived in the Christian Faith and Life Community in Austin, Texas, from 1957–59, attended Harvard Divinity School, and has been actively involved in the Northern Student Movement, the Southern Students' Organizing Committee, Students for a Democratic Society (SDS), and Student Nonviolent Coordinating Committee (SNCC).

MARY DALY is Associate Professor of Theology at Boston College. She is author of *The Church and the Second Sex* (Harper & Row, 1968) and the recently published *Beyond God the Father: Toward a Philosophy of Women's Liberation* (Beacon Press, 1973). She has written numerous articles and speaks to various groups across the country on the subject of the women's revolution.

ALICE L. HAGEMAN was Lentz Lecturer on Women and Ministry at Harvard Divinity School during 1972–73, and coordinated the series of lectures on which this book is based. Co-editor of *Religion in Cuba Today* (Association Press, 1971), she is currently working part-time as Liturgist at the Church of the Covenant in Boston, developing non-sexist expressions of faith and celebration. After receiving her M.Div. from Union Theological Seminary in 1962, she represented the World Student Christian Federation at UNESCO in Paris (1962–65), where she developed a lively interest in the relation between the church and international issues. She became involved in the women's movement in

1969 through the "women's caucus" of the committee of Returned Volunteers in New York City.

BEVERLY WILDUNG HARRISON is Associate Professor of Christian Ethics at Union Theological Seminary. Her current interests are contemporary theological ethics, social theory, and American political problems. Much of her recent work has been on the importance of feminism for these issues. She is a member of a working group currently writing a book on the feminist perspective on Christian ministry.

THERESSA HOOVER is Associate General Secretary, Women's Division, Board of Global Ministries of the United Methodist Church. She is also Chairperson of the National YWCA Committee on Racial Justice, member of the World Council of Churches Commission on the Churches' Participation in Development and writes a monthly feature for *response*, the official magazine for United Methodist Women. She currently serves as a member of the General Board of the National Council of Churches.

NELLE MORTON is at present an Associate Professor Emeritus of The Theological School of Drew University, Madison, New Jersey, where she taught for sixteen years. She is devoting her time to lecturing and writing on the women's movement. Formerly she was Executive Secretary of the Fellowship of Southern Churchmen.

GWEN KENNEDY NEVILLE is Assistant Professor of Anthropology at Emory University, Atlanta, Georgia, and member of the faculty, Division of Religion. She is currently advising a women students' coalition, serving on several university and professional association committees on women's issues, writing and speaking on women and culture, and consulting as a workshop leader with corporations on women in the professional world. Her research interests include education and culture, religion and culture, European ethnic groups in the United States (including white Protestants); among her other interests are three children ages twelve, ten, and nine, and one husband who is a counseling psychologist.

LETTY M. RUSSELL is Assistant Professor of Religious Studies at Manhattan College, Bronx, New York. She has also taught at Union Theological Seminary, New York Theological Seminary, Yale Divinity School, and Union Theological College, Bangalore, India. She served for three years as Religious Consultant to the National Board of the YWCA and for ten years as a pastor of the Presbyterian Church of the Ascension of the East Harlem Protestant Parish, New York City. She was a member of the first graduating class which included women at Harvard Divinity School.

GAIL SHULMAN received her A.B. from Connecticut College in 1969. She is presently a third-year student in the M. Div. program at Harvard Divinity School and a member of the Women's Caucus. Her article was originally submitted as a final project for a course, "Women and Religion in Sexist Society."

KRISTER STENDAHL is Dean of Harvard Divinity School, and author of *The Bible and the Role of Women* (Fortress Press, 1966).